Report

Beyond Left and Right: Finding Consensus on Economic Inequality

Hannah Rich

Contents

Acknowledgements	5
This report in 30 seconds	7
Executive summary	9
Introduction	13
1. Why inequality matters	23
2. What theology has to say	34
3. Biblical context	46
4. Theology of inequality through the ages	61
5. Policy implications and recommendations	75
6. Conclusion	96

Acknowledgements

I would like to thank my Theos colleagues for their support throughout this research. In particular, Madeleine Pennington, Simon Perfect and Pete Whitehead who facilitated the roundtables and helped draw together the myriad fascinating ideas into a coherent report, and Nick Spencer, Paul Bickley and Nathan Mladin who provided feedback on various drafts.

This report would also not have been possible without the contributions and encouragement of the roundtable participants, who were all unfailingly generous with both time and wisdom. A particular mention goes to Jeremy Williams and Roger Haydon Mitchell for their introductory presentations.

I also want to pay tribute to the late Professor Sir John Hills, who supervised my master's thesis at the LSE Inequalities Institute and encouraged my interest in this field. His work on intractable social policy challenges like inequality was invaluable and his voice in this conversation is greatly missed.

Lastly, thank you to the Douglas Trust for its continued generosity in funding this project.

Hannah Rich, September 2021

This report in 30 seconds

Economic inequality is a growing concern in politics and our public conversations, both globally and nationally – but it is often seen as a divisive or partisan issue, and there is little agreement on what (if anything) we ought to do about it. Bringing together academics and practitioners from a range of political and disciplinary backgrounds in a series of roundtables, Theos sought to build consensus around the extent to which economic inequality is a problem.

We found agreement that the impact of excessive and/or widening inequality is as evident in our relationships as in our bank balances. Inequalities of wealth and income have consequences for the way we view both ourselves and others. This report argues that prioritising flourishing human relationships should be the primary criteria for any approach to addressing economic inequality in policy and practice. It explores how the discipline of theology, and in particular that of Christianity, is well positioned to shape our moral imaginations to work towards greater economic – and relational – equality.

Executive summary

Economic inequality is one of the defining issues of our time, both within countries and across the globe, and has gained political salience and public attention in recent years. However, measures to address it are often made difficult by the divisive and partisan nature of the problem, which hinders any consensus on how we ought to go about reducing inequality.

In this report, we contend that theology offers a different way of exploring excessive economic inequality, and can open up new avenues of consensus between political and social positions that have typically been at odds.

With respect to economic inequality, we argue that:

— Inequality is not only an economic problem, but a social and relational one too. Absolute equality of wealth and income is neither achievable nor necessarily desirable, but both the causes and consequences of excessive inequality are concerning and should be tackled.

— Excessive inequality is both a cause and a symptom of societal dysfunction, such as the deeper power imbalance between those with and without resources.

— Inequality is especially concerning when it undermines our capacity to have good relationships with one another and separates us from community. The line at which inequality becomes excessive is as much a feeling as it is an economic or material reality.

— There are ecological as well as economic reasons to be concerned about inequality.

Regarding the role of theology, we then argue that:

- It underlines the importance of human relationships and how they are affected by inequality. Humans are fundamentally dependent on a network of relationships to flourish and make meaning; inequality is harmful where it prevents this flourishing.
- A theological perspective gives us the moral imagination to acknowledge that the world is not the way it should be.
- The practical engagement of faith communities with the symptoms of inequality, through social action, gives them legitimacy in speaking about the harms it causes.
- There are specific theological principles from throughout history that have much to contribute to our contemporary economic understanding, even for those who do not share the Judeo-Christian tradition. For example, the Old Testament idea of Jubilee can shape our approach to debt, accumulation and wealth. Additionally, the theological imperative to love our neighbours provides a helpful framework for understanding our duty to others, both locally, nationally and globally.

We then outline various policy solutions and means of addressing economic inequality that we suggest are most likely to draw consensus across political tribes.

- If inequality is a relational problem, then relational solutions are important. We begin from the position that people are not merely economic equations to be fixed or inequalities to be levelled up, but potential to be developed.
- We propose that improving cohesion between people of different backgrounds is key to addressing the social consequences of inequality, whether through

community projects or educational programmes like a national citizen scheme. Shared public spaces and better infrastructure can also engender more equal relationships with communities.

— Policy initiatives that support stable households may reduce economic inequality too, not least because of the improved health and educational outcomes associated with stable relationships.

— There is also a role for business and the market in addressing inequality. We suggest that pay ratios between employees could achieve this, along with reorienting our economy towards co-operative models and worker-led democracy.

— While the size and role of the state in mediating economic inequality is disputed, we argue that greater investment in support services and adult education would address some of the causes of inequality. The model of universal basic services could shape this.

— Taxation can reinforce the social dynamic of the economy, as well as the theological principle that wealth is temporary and should be held lightly. We identify greater openness to previously disputed forms of this, such as a wealth tax, in light of the pandemic.

— Together with specific policy proposals, there is also scope for reimagining our economic models. We suggest that a Christian approach to inequality would mean recalibrating the economy to prioritise wellbeing, without disregarding economic growth completely.

Introduction

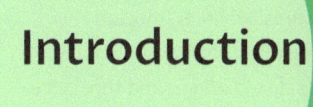

In the post-pandemic agenda, 'levelling up' has emerged as Westminster's favoured economic buzzphrase. This draws on the notion that many people and communities across the UK have been left behind, and thus require targeted measures to rebalance or 'level up' the disparity between them and wealthier areas.[1] It is at the heart of the narrative around the so-called "Red Wall" – the swathe of constituencies in the Midlands and North of England that were traditional Labour heartlands but increasingly vote Conservative and supported Leave in the EU referendum.

In his first speech as Prime Minister, Boris Johnson employed the language of levelling up in outlining plans to boost economic performance outside of London and rebalance regional disparities.[2] This appeared to pay dividends for Johnson's party in the 2019 General Election, which saw the expansion of Conservative support in areas it had not traditionally held. In its Spending Review in March 2021, the government announced a Levelling Up fund of £4.8 billion to support town centre regeneration, local transport and cultural heritage in areas characterised as being 'left behind'.[3] This was instrumental in the Hartlepool by-election two months later, in which the Conservatives won a seat that had been held by Labour for over sixty years.[4] In September 2021, the government reiterated this commitment by renaming the Ministry of Housing, Communities and Local Government to be the Department for Levelling Up, Housing and Communities.[5]

Levelling up the country is a governmental priority for good reason. Research by the Institute for Fiscal Studies (IFS) found that the UK is one of the most geographically unequal countries in the developed world. However, the IFS research cautioned against a simplistic approach to redressing these disparities, stating that "the UK's regional inequalities are deep-rooted and complex," such that successful policy approaches should be "long-term and multifaceted".[6] It also noted that so-called 'left-behind' places are not all the same in character, nor will they react uniformly to the joint economic challenges of Brexit and Covid-19.

The disparities implied by the need to 'level up' are the geographic manifestation of high economic inequality in the UK. This is not an altogether new phenomenon, but has become a key paradigm in social science and policymaking in recent years. A search in Hansard shows an approximately tenfold increase in the appearance of the word "inequality" in transcripts of Westminster parliamentary debates between 1970 and 2020.[7] The UK is the 20th most unequal country of 38 in the OECD before taxes and transfers but rises to the 7th most unequal once these are factored in.[8] This suggests the current political programme is, and has long been, inefficient at redistributing income.

Even the Church is not immune from geographical inequalities. A motion proposed to the Church of England's General Synod in early 2021 called for the levelling up of financial inequities between dioceses. It highlighted that diocesan wealth ranges from 95p per capita in the poorest dioceses to £92 in the richest, often coinciding with poorer and richer communities.[9] This is underscored by historical legacies that have entrenched inequality between communities both within and without the structures of the Church. The motion was not ultimately debated, but the Bishop of Burnley, Philip North, said that "every time we [the Church] name and condemn inequality in our nation, our moral case is undermined by the gross inequalities that exist within our common life."[10]

> **Economic inequality has gained salience as a policy issue to a perhaps unprecedented extent, and public attitudes are beginning to reflect this.**

A survey by researchers at King's College London (KCL) in late 2020 found almost two thirds of Britons (62%) believed that Britain was either somewhat or very unequal prior to the pandemic, compared with just one in eight (12%) who thought it was relatively equal.[11] Nonetheless, this was split along party lines, with Labour voters more likely than Conservative ones to perceive the country as unequal, and Remain voters more likely than Leave ones.

Whether organically or due to the prevailing rhetoric, the need to address perceived geographical inequalities has captured public attention. Geographical inequality was the form of inequality on which the KCL researchers found the strongest cross-party consensus; it was seen as a serious concern by 61% of all groups, 67% of Labour voters and 59% of Conservative voters.[12] This underscores the popularity of 'levelling up'. (Participants were asked to pick up to four types of inequality, from a possible eight, which they thought were "the most serious in Britain".)

Inequalities of wealth and income also emerged as a concern, although attitudes here were more clustered around partisan identity. While 60% overall saw this as an issue – in line with the 61% who identified geographical inequalities – this split into 53% of Conservative and 72% of Labour voters.[13]

The consensus here is striking compared to other issues; 61% of the population represents greater support than that of either side on Brexit. By contrast, 45% thought inequalities of race and ethnicity were among the most serious concerns, 28% identified inequalities between genders, and less than a quarter (22%) agreed that inequality between generations was one of the most significant issues. Perhaps most strikingly of all, given the KCL polling was undertaken during a pandemic that laid these inequities bare, only 26% of the public thought that unequal outcomes in health and life expectancy were one of the most serious types of inequality in Britain today.[14]

> **While there is consensus that economic inequality is an issue, potential solutions draw more partisan-based support.**

It seems, therefore, that there is broad public agreement that economic inequality is a significant enough issue to merit concerted action. However, as inequality activist and writer Ben Phillips describes, there is also a paradox in which "the mainstream consensus has shifted to recognise the inequality crisis without a consequent sufficient shift in action."[15]

This is partly because **while there is consensus that economic inequality is an issue, potential solutions draw more partisan-based support and it is thus harder to build a coalition around how – and even whether – we should tackle it.**

How proposed interventions are framed is therefore crucial. In the same KCL research, 62% of the public thought the government should "take measures to reduce income differences".[16] Yet when the question was phrased in terms of whether the government should "redistribute income from the better off to those who are less well off", only 48% agreed.

This difference was starker among Conservative voters: 46% agreed with the reduction of income differences (compared with 81% of Labour), but only 26% agreed with income redistribution (73% Labour). The same pattern is true on both sides of the Brexit divide; 53% of Leave voters and 72% of Remain voters agreed with reducing income differences, while 38% of Leave and 53% of Remain supported income redistribution. **Support for measures to address inequality increases when they are not presented as explicit forms of redistribution,** particularly among Conservative voters. This is crucial to recognise if a consensus is to be achieved.

Globally, economic growth and poverty reduction have been successful to the extent that nowadays, particularly in richer countries, inequality is caused less by the scarcity of resources that once prevailed and more by their inequitable distribution. Social geographer Danny Dorling describes this situation as resulting from "the wrong answer to the question of what to do now we are rich."[17] The UK is the world's sixth largest economy, yet 31% of children are growing up in poverty, three quarters of whom live in a household where at least one person works.[18]

We contend that Dorling's question – "what to do now?" – and its response are not only matters of economics, but have a moral and spiritual side too.

With this in mind, through a consensus-building process across different political and religious perspectives, this report therefore explores how bringing theological resources to bear on current debates can lead us to ask different questions of ourselves and of our dominant economic models – and how in turn this can influence our approach to economic inequality. The aim of this report is not to articulate a definitive Christian perspective on contemporary economic policy, but rather to derive some principles from theology that might bridge apparent gaps and shape a cross-partisan response to inequality.

As a discipline, theology is often neglected by the world of policy. It is the study of ultimate meaning, through understanding God and God's relation to the world, and of religious practice and experience. But more broadly, it grapples deeply with questions of human identity, relationships, and what we owe one another – and has been seeking the answers to these questions for thousands of years. This approach – trying a different starting point in order to bring us to more constructive answers – leads us to consider what theologian Duncan Forrester called "the human meaning of inequality"; that is, the experience and significance of inequality for human beings rather than in abstracted economic terms.[19] Understanding this dimension compels us to view potential policy interventions to tackle inequality in light of their human significance.

Methodology

This report is informed by three online roundtables we held on the theme of economic inequality. The fifteen participants included theologians, economists, policy analysts, local politicians, think tank professionals, charity workers, and church leaders. These were chosen to represent a breadth of professional experience, as well as a range of political and religious positions.

The purpose was to bring together the voices of those who might typically have disagreed about the causes of (and potential solutions to) economic inequality, and thus to move the discussion about inequality beyond the left-right political divide. In doing so, we recognised that **solving economic inequality is not only about the legitimacy of state redistribution of wealth, but encompasses many of our most basic intuitions about human dignity and community.** The roundtable conversations were designed to provoke discussion and disagreement but also to unearth unexpected points of consensus between participants.

The roundtables were held under the Chatham House rule and therefore we do not identify participants. However, their contributions were fundamental to the research process. Where a particular point arose from the roundtables, this is acknowledged.

We were inspired in this approach by the AEI-Brookings Institution working group on child poverty, which enabled policy makers on the left and right to come together on this issue. Their work spanned fourteen months and involved fifteen politically diverse thinkers, "drawing on principles designed to maximize civility, trust, and open-mindedness".[20] The chair, New York University social psychologist Jonathan Haidt, acknowledged the value of the exercise in challenging people from different viewpoints to agree with each other and consider views they might usually dismiss.[21] We sought to model this in our smaller-scale consensus-building process.

1. BBC News, 'What is levelling up and how is going?' *BBC News* (2021). Available at: www.bbc.co.uk/news/56238260

2. Prime Minister's Office, *Boris Johnson's first speech as Prime Minister*, 24 July 2019. Available at: www.gov.uk/government/speeches/boris-johnsons-first-speech-as-prime-minister-24-july-2019

3. HM Treasury, *Levelling Up Fund: Prospectus*. (HM Treasury: London, 2021). Available at: www.gov.uk/government/publications/levelling-up-fund-prospectus

4. Bhattacharya, A., *So now you give a monkey's? The policy wonk's guide to Hartlepool.* (London: Social Market Foundation, 2021). Available at: www.smf.co.uk/publications/policy-guide-to-hartlepool/

5. UK Government. *Press Release: Ambitious plans to drive levelling up agenda.* (UK Government, 2021). Available at: www.gov.uk/government/news/ambitious-plans-to-drive-levelling-up-agenda

6. Davenport, A. and Zaranko, B., 'Levelling Up: Where and How', I*FS Green Budget 2020.* (London: Institute for Fiscal Studies, 2020). Available at: www.ifs.org.uk/uploads/CH7-IFS-Green-Budget-2020-Levelling-up.pdf

7. Search conducted using Hansard data, available online.

8. OECD, *Income inequality* (indicator), 2021. Available at: data.oecd.org/inequality/income-inequality.htm

9. Davies, M., 'Bishop of Sheffield: Let the rich dioceses be generous to poorer ones'. *Church Times*, 28 May 2021. Available at: www.churchtimes.co.uk/articles/2021/28-may/news/uk/bishop-of-sheffield-let-the-rich-dioceses-be-generous-to-poorer-ones

10. Thornton, E., 'Sheffield trauma will not be revisited'. *Church Times*, 9 July 2021. Available at: www.churchtimes.co.uk/articles/2021/16-july/news/uk/sheffield-trauma-will-not-be-revisited-synod-hears

11. Duffy, B., Hewlett, K., Hesketh, R., Benson, R. and A. Wager, *Unequal Britain: Attitudes to inequalities after Covid-19.* (London: King's College, 2021), p.13. Available at: www.kcl.ac.uk/policy-institute/assets/unequal-britain.pdf

12. Duffy et al. , *Unequal Britain*, p. 5.

13. Duffy et al., *Unequal Britain*, p. 16.

14. Duffy et al., *Unequal Britain*, p. 15.

15. Phillips, B., *How to Fight Inequality and Why That Fight Needs You*. (Cambridge: Polity Press, 2020), p.8.

16. Duffy et al., *Unequal Britain*, p. 58.

17 Dorling, D, Injustice: *Why Social Inequality Persists*. (Bristol: Policy Press, 2010), p.1.

18 Child Poverty Action Group, *Child Poverty Facts and Figures*, March 2021. Available at: cpag.org.uk/child-poverty/child-poverty-facts-and-figures

19 Forrester, D, On Human Worth: A Christian Vindication of Equality. (London: SCM Press, 2001), p.20.

20 American Enterprise Institute for Public Policy Research and the Brookings Institution, *Opportunity, Responsibility and Security: A Consensus Plan for Reducing Poverty and Restoring the American Dream*. (Washington DC: AEI/Brookings, 2015). Available at: www.brookings.edu/wp-content/uploads/2016/07/full-report.pdf

21 Haidt, J., 'Two incompatible sacred values in American universities (text)', *Hayek Lecture Series, Duke University*, 2016. Available at: theindependentwhig.com/haidt-passages/haidt/haidt-two-incompatible-sacred-values-in-american-universities/

1.
Why inequality matters

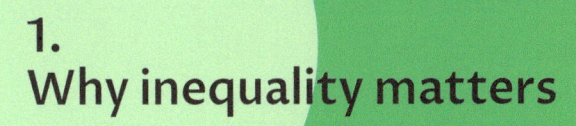

To reach a consensus across perspectives on reducing economic inequality, we must begin with a shared understanding of whether (and why) the issue matters at all, both morally and materially. In our first roundtable conversation, we addressed the questions of whether we should all be equal and what level of economic inequality might be considered excessive. Whilst participants agreed that absolute economic equality was not the right goal, we found consensus around the idea that excessive economic inequality is a problem, with damaging moral and social consequences.

Should we all be equal?

The notion that economic inequality is a problem to be tackled can be misinterpreted as suggesting that we should strive for complete equality in economic terms. This is a significant barrier to building consensus across political divides on this issue. If the end goal of inequality reduction is perceived to be perfect equality, it is easy to stereotype any effort to reduce inequality as tantamount to communism, and it quickly becomes politically alienating. Moving away from these divisive caricatures is thus critical. This begins with the acknowledgement that **absolute equality of wealth and income is neither achievable nor necessarily desirable.**

When measuring income inequality by the Gini coefficient, a coefficient of zero indicates a population in which all values are the same, i.e. where everyone has exactly the same income. Conversely, a coefficient of one indicates the opposite, whereby one individual has the entire income and the rest of the population has none. The coefficient can be calculated with respect to forms of either income or wealth, but in all cases, these extremes are hypothetical. Even at the height of the socialist regime, the estimated Gini coefficient on gross income of the Soviet Union did not fall below 0.2.[1] The Nordic countries viewed as paragons of equality currently have coefficients around 0.25 after taxes and transfers are applied.[2]

We heard agreement among roundtable participants that some degree of inequality is both natural and morally acceptable, and even necessary to preserve economic freedom in a society, for example, where inequality occurs through reasonable difference in effort or comparative difficulty of jobs.

Absolute equality of wealth and income is neither achievable nor necessarily desirable.

One hypothetical example given was the extreme scenario of a world in which all inequality could be attributed to inequality of effort. This would mean a society with initial equality of opportunity and value, but where citizens took advantage of this to differing degrees so that substantive equalities emerged. It was felt that it would be difficult to argue this situation was unacceptable or worth remedying, at least as long as such inequalities were not then inherited by the next generation, even if the inequality involved was great enough to be considered excessive otherwise.

This highlights the difference between inequality and injustice. Inequality refers to the unequal distribution of resources and opportunities within a population, whereas injustice or inequity specifically denotes a lack of fairness. Conceptually, inequality is a more quantitative and measurable category and is therefore favoured in economics, whereas injustice is more qualitative and normative. It was suggested that injustice is a less politically polarising term than inequality and that it might be easier to 'win' the public argument around inequality by framing injustice as the core issue. The language of seeking fairness or justice is less susceptible to caricatures about communism than that of equality can be, and the policies it leads to may well address inequality anyway. It is hard to conceive of an intervention aimed at addressing economic injustice that would not also tackle the greatest excesses of economic inequality.

Causes of inequality

The case of inequality of effort highlights how participants were concerned about the causes of economic inequality. It is therefore crucial to grasp the dynamics that drive inequality, not only the measured level of it. In this regard, Thomas Piketty is justified in describing the Gini coefficient as offering "an abstract and sterile view of inequality".[3] Two populations could have the same measured level of inequality, with vastly different factors driving it. It is possible, for example, for the majority of the population to be equally poor rather than equally wealthy. This also does not take into account the political regime that may affect inequality in a country. Indeed, the moral acceptability of economic equality might depend on whether it had been enforced coercively, or emerged through nudging policies and people's natural behaviour.

To some, economic inequality matters when and because it is indicative of injustice. The dynamics behind inequality may also be issues of social justice, and these are often deep-rooted and historically reinforced. Contemporary inequality can be the result of historical injustice; for example, wealth that is accumulated by unjust means then passed on through inheritance, reinforcing a lottery of birth that undermines the capacity of individual effort to achieve equal reward.

Inheritance also works detrimentally in the other direction; 45% of UK earnings inequalities are passed on generationally.[4] Differences in how the taxation system treats wealth and income further entrench this.

Implications of inequality

If the causes of inequality are a key reason for concern, then its implications are another. Social scientists have drawn a correlation between economic inequality and all manner of social ills including reduced social mobility[5], reduced levels of trust within society[6], educational disadvantage[7], and accelerated climate change.[8] Most famously, Richard Wilkinson and Kate Pickett's *The Spirit Level* suggested that more equal societies perform better on a range of socioeconomic metrics and that inequality is directly responsible for negative outcomes. Public health expert Sir Michael Marmot claims that poor health outcomes are causally related to higher economic inequality.[9]

These assertions are not without their critics; some have questioned the strength of this causal relationship between inequality and social problems, and pointed out the selectiveness of the evidence.[10] Yet even those sceptical of the Spirit Level hypothesis acknowledge that such outcomes signal underlying problems and are symptomatic of a society not functioning as it should.

Excessive inequality is both a cause and a symptom of societal dysfunction, such as the deeper power imbalance between those with and without resources.

Economist Joseph Stiglitz argues that inequality is a result of political and economic power being concentrated in the hands of the few, leading to divisions in society that, he says, endanger our common future.[11] This is evident in the high levels of violent crime in cities like São Paulo, where extreme economic inequality plays out with grave consequences for physical security.[12] Brazil is the third most unequal country in the world and the social harm of this is heightened by the close physical proximity of the richest and poorest.

There are also environmental reasons to be concerned about economic inequality; overconsumption of planetary resources is an increasingly urgent ecological and economic concern. The "doughnut economics" model developed by economist Kate Raworth is instructive here, arguing that there is a floor below which individuals lack access to life's essentials and an ecological ceiling beyond which planetary resources become unsustainable.[13] She calls the space in between, where both the needs of humanity and those of the planet are met, the "doughnut" and suggests that a sustainable economy is one where we all live within that space. Designing our economic system around this space requires a fairer distribution of planetary resources.

As humans, we are part of the natural world and subject to ecological crises, which is a pragmatic rather than primarily ideological reason to ameliorate inequalities that are harmful to the planet and to our neighbours. The effects of climate change are felt disproportionately in the majority world, deepening long-existent inequalities.[14] Addressing inequality requires us to both improve the life chances of the very poorest and restrain the excesses of the very rich, since to do one without the other would overstretch the planet's limited resources. It has been estimated that if the entire global population lived like the USA, we would need five planets to accommodate it. The UK requires the equivalent of 3.9 United Kingdoms to meet its residents' demand on nature.[15]

Inequality and relationships

Living within the 'doughnut' in economic terms also has implications for how we relate to each other. Over the course of our roundtables, we found striking consensus that, above all, **inequality becomes a problem when it undermines our capacity to have good relationships with one another and separates us from community.** Sharp economic inequalities can be damaging to the social fabric of a society, undermining collective solidarity and sacrifice. Where wealth flows towards the top, this creates social divisions and can lead to the erosion of democracy.

Many of the factors that Wilkinson and Pickett associate with greater inequality, such as reduced trust and cohesion, pertain to relationships and social connections. Income and wealth are proxies valued by society in which we see other inequalities reflected. We are better able to measure these factors, **but focusing only on economic metrics can lead us to miss the fundamental problem of how we are connected to each other within society.**

Drawing on the work of network sociologist Harrison White, who analysed the patterns of social relations within a society, Mike Savage writes that:

The awareness of inequality ultimately derives from the contingency of recognising that you are different from others. It is when we feel that a particular script does not, and cannot, apply to us, that difference slides into inequality. This stuff – this feeling – of inequality is historically tied up with the formation of social groups and identities.[16]

This illustrates how **the line at which inequality becomes excessive is as much a feeling as it is an economic or material reality.** This sentiment is what drives the social consequences; the feeling of being unequal has profound psychological implications, individually and collectively. If inequality undermines emotional solidarity, then addressing it is good for us all. We might suggest that self-interest and morality come together in the case for tackling inequalities and this is a helpful recognition in the search for consensus across politics.[17]

> **If inequality undermines emotional solidarity, then addressing it is good for us all.**

Summary

Whilst different roundtable participants had different tolerance levels for economic inequality, we found a clear consensus that there is a point at which inequality becomes excessive and is therefore morally problematic. We can consider the harms generated by excessive inequality and therefore deem it worthy of rectifying without suggesting we should all be completely equal. Rather than seeking complete equality, our efforts would be better spent controlling excessive inequality. The question is where to draw this line.

Excessive inequality is a greater moral concern than the existence of inequality at all, and is particularly intolerable when people feel that it cannot be addressed effectively. The harms of excessive inequality are distinct from the morality of an individual having too much. Inequality is wrong at a corporate level when (and because) it leads to societal dysfunction, as well as when it undermines our capacity to respond adequately to the ecological and climate crises.

Economic inequality is about how we value others within society; equality of value is something for which we might aim. Absolute economic equality is not the end goal, but greater economic equality is an important indicator that we are moving in the direction of greater human flourishing.

1. Alexeev, M. and Gaddy, C., 'Income Distribution in the USSR in the 1980s', *Review of Income and Wealth*, Series 39, No. 1, (1993), p.29.

2. Gini coefficient data as calculated by World Bank, 2020.

3. Piketty, T., *Capital in the Twenty-First Century* Translated by A. Goldhammer. (Cambridge, MA: Harvard University Press, 2014), p. 334.

4. Friedman, S., Laurison, D. and Macmillan, L., *Social Mobility, the Class Pay Gap and Intergenerational Worklessness: New Insights from The Labour Force Survey* (London: Social Mobility Commission and LSE, 2017). Available at: www.lse.ac.uk/business/consulting/reports/social-mobility-the-class-pay-gap-and-intergenerational-worklessness

5. Wilkinson, R. and Pickett, K., *The Spirit Level: Why Equality is Better for Everyone* (London: Penguin, 2009).

6. Uslaner, E., *The Moral Foundations of Trust* (Cambridge: Cambridge University Press, 2002).

7. Hills, J., McKnight, A., Bucelli, I., Karagiannaki, E., Vizard, P., Yang, L., Duque, M. and Rucci, M., *Understanding the Relationship Between Poverty and Inequality: Overview Report* (London: Centre for Analysis of Social Exclusion, LSE, 2019), pp. 69-70. Available at: sticerd.lse.ac.uk/dps/case/cr/casereport119.pdf

8. Borunda, A., 'Inequality is decreasing between countries – but climate change is slowing progress'. *National Geographic*, 22, (2019). Available at: www.nationalgeographic.com/environment/2019/04/climate-changeeconomic-inequality-growing/

9. Marmot, M., 'Social determinants of health inequalities', *Lancet*, 365, (2005), pp. 1099-1104.

10. Saunders, P., *Beware False Prophets: Equality, the Good Society and The Spirit Level* (London: Policy Exchange, 2010). Available at: www.policyexchange.org.uk/wp-content/uploads/2016/09/beware-false-prophets-jul-10.pdf; see also Hassan, G., 'The Fantasyland of 'The Spirit Level' and the Limitations of the Health and Well-Being Industry'. *OpenDemocracy*, 2010. Available at: www.opendemocracy.net/en/opendemocracyuk/fantasyland-of-spirit-level-and-limitations-of-health-and-well-being-indu

11. Stiglitz, J., *The Price of Inequality: How Today's Divided Society Endangers Our Future* (New York: W.W. Norton & Company, 2012).

12. Caldeira, T., *City of Walls: Crime, Segregation, and Citizenship in São Paulo* (Berkeley, CA: University of California Press, 2001.)

13. Raworth, K., *Doughnut Economics: Seven Ways to Think Like a 21st-Century Economist* (London: Random House, 2017.)

14 Mendelsohn. R, Dinar, A. and Williams, L., 'The Distributional Impact of Climate Change on Rich and Poor Countries'. *Environment and Development Economics* 11:02, (2006), pp. 1–20.

15 Data from Earth Overshoot Day, available at: www.overshootday.org/how-many-earths-or-countries-do-we-need/

16 Savage, M., *The Return of Inequality: Social Change and the Weight of the Past* (Cambridge, MA: Harvard University Press, 2021), p. 168.

17 Hicks, D., 'How Economic Inequality is a Theological and Moral Issue', *Interpretation: A Journal of Bible and Theology,* Volume 69, Issue 4, (2015), pp. 432-446.

2.
What theology has to say

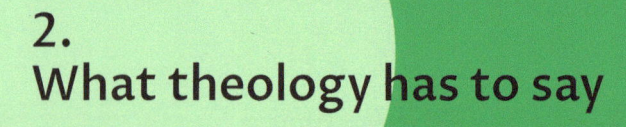

In her essay collection on money and culture, *Having and Being Had*, American writer Eula Biss tells a story about her struggling neighbour who, when circumstances conspire against him, concludes with a smile that it must be divine will: "I guess God, he says, doesn't want me to have money."[1] This anecdote is presented in jest, but reflects the notion of an unjust divine economy with which many wrestle – a sort of theological and financial karma. It suggests the common view that belief in God implies either the passive acceptance of injustice, or living at the mysterious whims of a despotic supernatural ruler. Yet for most Christians, this is far from their vision of faith.

In this chapter, we explore why theology as a discipline might be a valuable conversation partner for economic debates about inequality, before proceeding to explore the Bible and other theological texts in greater depth in subsequent chapters.

As noted above, a strong sense emerged through our roundtables that human relationships and flourishing should be central to the discussion about excessive economic inequality. What we are lacking in this conversation is not hard economic facts, but the moral imagination to address them – and at its best, **theology has the capacity to shape this imagination, speaking to the value of these relationships, and how we nurture them, without becoming too idealistic or abstract.**

For most of human history, religious traditions have been a primary means of navigating the world, including questions of economics, yet this aspect has all but disappeared from the contemporary conversation. Perhaps it is arrogant to think that theology no longer has anything to contribute; might it still help us mediate economic dilemmas like that posed by excessive inequality?

In grappling with questions of ultimate meaning, theology cannot avoid contending with the fundamental nature of humanity, in all its complexity. This entails understanding the reality of human brokenness and the difficulty of creating a just society within the constraints of this imperfect reality. It also means taking into account the value of humans beyond what is acknowledged in secular society, as beings created "in the image of God".

Theology can therefore offer an alternative story of human worth, encompassing the tension and imperfection of the world as it is and the hope of how it should, and will, be. It is concerned with trying to understand and realise God's will for humanity and pursue human dignity. It offers a broad holistic understanding of what enables human beings and creation to flourish, as well as what diminishes flourishing and restricts our agency to realise our full potential. The conception of who we are as humans made in the 'image and likeness of God', through the lens of theology – referred to as Christian theological anthropology – can shape our fundamental understanding of humanity.

Below we consider some principles of Christian theology that have particular pertinence in debates around economic inequality.

> **Theology can therefore offer an alternative story of human worth, encompassing the tension and imperfection of the world as it is and the hope of how it should, and will, be.**

That relationships matter

It was highlighted in the roundtables that Christian theology emphasises the idea of equality within community, without subverting the differences that do exist. Two theological motifs were used to illustrate this: firstly, the Trinity and secondly, the body of Christ.

The Christian God is understood as a Trinity, which is the idea that God is three persons in one – the Father, the Son and the Holy Spirit – and fundamentally represents unity within community. Each person within the Trinity is distinctive, but shares in the same divine essence, and has full agency and equality. The community of the Trinity itself could not flourish without this. This view of God affirms that not only are relationships important, but the ultimate fabric of reality itself is relationship. This is known in theological terms as 'perichoresis', which describes the interpersonal relationship of the Trinity.[2]

If, as Christians believe, humans are made in the image of God, then the intrinsic interrelatedness of the Trinity should inform our understanding of human relationships. Humans are fundamentally dependent on a network of relationships to flourish and make meaning; inequality is harmful where it prevents people flourishing in this way.

The metaphor of the people of God as like the parts of a body, expressed in 1 Corinthians 12, develops this. It expresses how people have different abilities and levels of wealth, yet all contribute together to the common Christian life. As has already been established, equality of value rather than absolute material equality is the goal here. Every individual should have full agency, without negating the different functions, capacities and potential each may possess.

That things are not as they should be

Christian theology also offers a profound recognition that, while equality of value is ultimately the truth of who we are, this is not the perfect reality we live in. As the Church of England's Ethical Investment Advisory Group acknowledges, for example, "when material rewards become vastly unequal, it becomes harder for people to perceive the truth of equality before God since it is contradicted by their experience of the world."[3]

A specifically Christian understanding uses the lens of what it would call "sin" as a focus for the behaviour that inequality causes and is caused by. Sin is understood as an offence against God, against his will and against our neighbours. Episcopal priest and theologian Fleming Rutledge makes this explicit in describing growing inequality in the USA as "the result of Sin in which our whole society participates".[4] If inequality is problematic because of the injustice it implies, then seeking justice rather than equality should be a priority. This brings with it the recognition of **how human sin is core to the injustices behind inequalities,** whether this sin is greed, selfishness, excessive consumption, the failure to care for each other or a lack of compassion.

Sin is not a common concept in secular economics, nor is it one that sits comfortably in non-religious conversations. However, theologians often talk about it in explicitly economic terms; for example, the idea that sin is a form of debt, as seen in the interchangeability of "forgive us our sins/trespasses/debts" in various translations of the Lord's Prayer.

Sin can be seen as putting 'I' before 'we', or as taking rather than sharing – both of which might also begin to describe the mechanisms by which inequality emerges in the economy. It is also helpful in examining our own individual and corporate culpability for inequality. As wealthy westerners, we are among "the world's small minority of extravagantly consuming people" and therefore find ourselves complicit in the "structural evils that oppose God's hope and love," even if unwittingly.[5]

While talking about sin may engender feelings of guilt, it is not always a bad emotion and in fact may be essential for bringing about positive change. It might be needed in order to motivate individuals to change their economic and environmental behaviour. **The language of sin, paradoxically, might also contain the hope of change.** If greed is seen as sinful, then by extension it is contrary to the natural order of things and thus there is hope of another way. This is preferable to seeing greed and the associated economic injustices as the inevitable, natural state of humanity, which can lead to complacency and failure to act.[6] It is precisely here that Christian theology forms a moral imagination compelling us to address inequality.

That we are all neighbours

The **theological concept of the neighbour** is another principle that Christians can offer to secular debates that set the local, national and global in tension with one another.

The command to love our neighbours may be undermined by large-scale inequality in a society, or conversely such inequality may be an indication that we are not living up to that imperative. Loving our neighbour means recognising the deep bonds we share with those around us, whether this means close acquaintances or the homeless person we walk past every day. These relationships of neighbourliness remind us of the equal value that is, or should be, conferred on all human beings – but the way we experience them can also highlight inequality.

Global neighbourliness also matters, at a time when rising nationalisms tell us to reject our responsibility to others around the world, often on economic grounds. Christian theology reminds us that neighbourliness is embodied and relational, but not constrained by proximity; we bear some moral responsibility to both the person next door and the person a thousand miles away. As civil rights activist Howard Thurman wrote, "every man is potentially every other man's neighbour".[7]

In a globalised world, our economic life is structured such that we are inextricably connected to people and communities thousands of miles away through their involvement in our production and supply chains, as well as through the ecological impact of our behaviour on the majority world. Our apparent inability to address tax havens is a result of this global nature of capital, with consequences for inequality. Where there are environmental reasons to be concerned about inequality (as outlined in the previous chapter), these are also heightened by a theological understanding of who our neighbours are. Christian ethicist Cynthia Moe-Lobeda describes loving our neighbours as an "ecological and economic vocation"[8] Unlike our predecessors, we must grapple with the knowledge not only that our actions have consequences for the lives of others, but also that we have ways of changing this more directly, whether by behavioural shifts or charitable giving. The global scale of inequality should concern us all; our inaction poses a greater moral challenge today than previously.

That justice is key

Finally, theology centres the vision that **God is a God of justice and therefore we have to talk about injustice within the conversation about inequality.** This chimes with the secular suggestion that inequity and injustice, not only inequality, matter, but underpins it with a deeper divine rationale for concern. Particularly within the liberation tradition, justice is seen as the primary function of the people of God.

Black liberation theologian James H Cone viewed the scandal of poverty and economic oppression as the only possible starting point for theology; anything else, he said, would be a contradiction of the purpose of scripture.[9] As we explore in the next chapter, this is central to the economic vision of both the Old Testament and of theologians throughout the ages.

That practical witness matters

Together with their theology, **the practical experience of faith communities** offers insight into inequality. Local faith communities across religions and denominations are prophetic spaces between community life, people's experiences and the ideas of theology. They often reflect a degree of socioeconomic diversity not always espoused by other community groups, allowing people of faith to speak across difference and address issues in a non-partisan way.[10] This is a valuable facet to the contribution of theology and faith to public economic life.

Even for secular bodies that do not share their theological convictions, **the practical engagement of faith communities with the symptoms of inequality is demonstrable.** A report from the National Churches Trust in 2020 found that church buildings create £12.4 billion in economic value every year, of which £10 billion is the "non-market value" of social and mental wellbeing contributed.[11] In 2017, 93% of Church of England churches were involved in some way in the provision of food banks, whether through volunteering or financial giving.[12]

Through social action, congregations and churches engage in the lived reality of poverty and inequality, at home and abroad, and thus deepen their first-hand understanding of the structural inequalities at play. This faith-based action affords faith communities a greater legitimacy in speaking about the harms of economic inequality, backing up their theological ideas with practice.

The particular case of religious orders provides a microcosm of how **power and equality work in community** and what that means for wider society. For example, some communities hold solidarity and equality of decision-making as central to their collective life, democratically allocating resources among community members from a common pool. Decisions are taken collectively, so that every member's needs are met sufficiently. This does not lead to absolute equality of possessions, because it reflects different needs, roles and individual gifts.

A monastic community might elect a leader who then has 'unequal' power, but is elected on the basis of being good at exercising it. Similarly, a collectively owned car might apparently benefit those with the ability to drive disproportionately, but the joint decision to buy it reinforces equality of value rather than undermining it. This is echoed in the book of Acts, as we will explore later, where the emphasis is not on absolute equality but on sharing resources so that no one is in need.

A similar example raised in the roundtables is that of the Bruderhof, an intentional Anabaptist Christian community who practice common ownership and eschew personal finances.[13] Like monastic communities, they started from the basis of their theology, pooling their resources and removing money from their priorities. This resulted in a very different lifestyle from prevailing economic models. Notably, theirs is a framework that Christians from many different denominations and political positions all describe as inspirational. Thus, **Christian community can model a form of equality** that accounts for the different gifts of those who contribute to the common life, despite the contradictions that emerge.

> **Faith-based action affords faith communities a greater legitimacy in speaking about the harms of economic inequality, backing up their theological ideas with practice.**

The expression of Christian theology through liturgy is also relevant. As 1 Corinthians 11 directs, Christian community ought to reflect its sacramental practice; what is practiced in worship should be echoed in the way the community acts outside of it and what it believes about human dignity. Many examples shared by roundtable participants illustrated how the way we gather for worship is a model of what it means to belong to the community of the church. This in turn forms and communicates something of our understanding of inequality and injustice.

Summary

Professor of economics and theology Mary Hirschfeld writes that theology "should not be used to shore up one side or the other of secular debates" around inequality.[14] Secular discussions are often polarised between viewing capitalism as either exploitation or liberation. While theology is not immune from falling into the same trap, it may offer a basis for consensus.

In concluding, we return to Savage's notion that tolerable differences become problematic inequality "when we feel that a particular script does not, and cannot, apply to us."[15] The script implied by the Christian story is one that must apply to everyone, or its message is invalidated. The good news of the gospel is universally accessible or else it is nothing.

The fundamental idea that we are all equal in the eyes of God may seem a high bar to set for our socioeconomic structures, but it is precisely when these structures diverge from the script that inequality deepens. Therein lies the challenge and opportunity of theology.

1. Biss, E., *Having and Being Had* (London: Faber & Faber Limited, 2021), p.10.

2. Stamatović, S., 'The Meaning of Perichoresis'. *Open Theology*, Vol. 2, No. 1, (2016).

3. Church of England, *Executive Remuneration: The Policy of the National Investing Bodies of the Church of England and the Advisory Paper of the Ethical Investment Advisory Group of the Church of England*, 2019, p. 8. Available at: www.churchofengland.org/sites/default/files/2019-11/Final%20EIAG%20paper_Exec%20Remuneration_Final.pdf

4. Rutledge, F., *The Crucifixion* (Grand Rapids, MI: Eerdmans Publishing, 2015), p.177.

5. Moe-Lobeda, C., Resisting Structural Evil: Love as Ecological-Economic Vocation (Minneapolis, MN: Fortress Press, 2013), p. XVII.

6. With thanks to Simon Perfect for this point.

7. Thurman, H., *Jesus and The Disinherited* (Boston, MA: Beacon Press, 1996 [1949]), p. 89.

8. Moe-Lobeda, C., *Resisting Structural Evil...*

9. Cone, J. H., *God of the Oppressed* (New York: Orbis Books, 1975), p.179.

10. Pennington, M., *The Church and Social Cohesion: Connecting Communities and Serving People* (London: Theos, 2020). Available at: www.theosthinktank.co.uk/cmsfiles/The-Church-and-Social-Cohesion.pdf

11. National Churches Trust, *The House of Good (London: National Churches Trust, 2020)*. Available at: www.houseofgood.nationalchurchestrust.org/

12. Church Urban Fund, *Church in Action: A National Survey* (London: Church Urban Fund, 2017). Available at: cuf.org.uk/resources/church-in-action-2017

13. Bruderhof, *Life in Community: Community of Goods.* (2021). Available at: www.bruderhof.com/en/life-in-community/community-of-goods

14. Hirschfeld, M., 'Rethinking economic inequality: a theological perspective', *Journal of Religious Ethics*, 47:2, (2019), p. 260.

15. Savage, M., *The Return of Inequality*, p.168.

3.
Biblical context

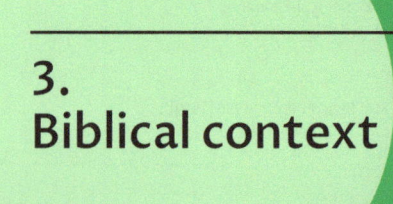

Having examined the broad ways in which some core theological principles can offer a helpful framework for analysing and addressing economic inequality, we now explore what the Christian tradition says more directly about economic inequality itself, beginning with the Bible.

Biblical teaching has been used widely to justify conflicting visions of the economy and of economic justice. Free marketeers and radical socialists, capitalists and liberation theologians, slave owners and abolitionists have all found in Christianity and, more specifically, in the Bible a basis and justification for their economic ideology.[1] The task of finding in the scriptures a coherent set of economic principles regarding inequality around which different political positions might coalesce therefore appears challenging.

Our aim is not to find a definitive 'biblical' position on contemporary economics. Rather, drawing on the roundtables, we hope to develop some principles which can underpin the beginnings of consensus between those of opposing political perspectives.

The Bible contains texts of different genres which each form part of the moral framework of the whole. Each genre also provides a different aspect of what scripture might say about inequality. For example, there are legal texts outlining the law of the Old Testament, prophetic texts speaking to the moral context and historical texts illustrating how these ideas worked in practice. Taking these as a starting point, we derive some principles from a combination of what is legislated (for or against), what is condemned, and what is modelled in the Bible. Each of these, and their intersections, has implications for how inequality might be addressed now.

What is legislated?

Firstly, we consider **what is legislated**. This does not mean that Old Testament legislation can or should be adopted wholesale into our own economic system. It does however offer a guide to determining the assumed role of legislation and the state in mitigating economic injustice. What a society opts to enshrine in law is a strong reflection of its priorities, as is also true of Old Testament Israel. The tendency towards wealth accumulation is not a modern phenomenon, as demonstrated by the Old Testament laws that address it as a growing trend, inferring that **it is right to have a means of correcting generational cycles of economic inequality and injustice**.

One of the Old Testament principles most explicitly concerned with governing the accumulation and just distribution of wealth is the institution of the Jubilee Year, which ordered the cancellation of debts and freeing of slaves every seven years, along with the redistribution of land every fifty years:

> *Count seven sabbath years – seven times seven years – so that the seven sabbath years amount to a period of forty-nine years. Then sound the trumpet everywhere on the tenth day of the seventh month; on the Day of Atonement sound the trumpet throughout your land. Consecrate the fiftieth year and proclaim liberty throughout the land to all its inhabitants. It shall be a jubilee for you... The fiftieth year shall be a jubilee for you; do not sow and do not reap what grows of itself or harvest the untended vines. For it is a jubilee and is to be holy for you; eat only what is taken directly from the fields. (Leviticus 25:8-12)*

Jubilee matters as a historical idea even for those who do not share its Judeo-Christian foundation. Academic and former Anglican priest Anthony Waterman, concludes that "all ethical consideration of inequality in the Christian West, and all political proposals for its cure, have their origin in the Levitical insight," such is the importance of this passage.[2]

As a motif for justice, the principle of Jubilee resonates beyond those who share the Christian faith. In the 1990s, it became a powerful and successful symbol for campaigners across the political and religious divides, calling for the cancellation of $90bn of debt owed by the world's poorest nations.[3] The same language has been employed more recently by secular commentators in the USA in relation to President Joe Biden's plans to forgive $400bn of student debt.[4]

Land denotes a foundational resource that affords individuals a stake in society. For our own non-agrarian, post-industrial society, we may interpret this as signifying that everyone should have the essential resources necessarily for full participation in society, as well as a basic livelihood. The book of Numbers (ch. 26-27) enshrines this importance of allocating land to afford every family a fair means of subsistence. Larger tribes were given more and allowances made for land quality to mediate the natural environment, ensuring equality of opportunity to pursue common economic life.

In a society like Old Testament Israel, where land was the primary source of sustenance, provision for its fair distribution was important to maintaining equality and "countering runaway inequality"[5]. It was "an institutionalised mechanism to prevent the kind of economic divisions where a few people would possess all the capital while others had no productive resources."[6] It represented a social ideal in which every household had enough land to meet its own needs and where "all had access to property and the means of production, debt-free, at least once during their adult lives."[7]

The Levitical law extends this to deal with what happens when a family loses its land, whether due to market failure, poor harvest or injustice, offering a mechanism for household economic recovery. The household thus remains a key economic unit and each is charged with stewardship of the land entrusted to it. This is important in distinguishing Jubilee ideologically from communism, because private wealth is neither condemned nor centralised.

As Jesuit priest Robert North put it, "where communism decrees, 'none shall have property', Leviticus decrees, 'none shall lose property'."[8] This shift in emphasis is significant in light of the propensity of the current debate to see pursuing equality as divisive or caricatured.

The principle of Jubilee institutionalises justice in a way that philanthropy does not and cannot. It applies equally to everyone and no one can evade it. It is "structured justice rather than mere charity."[9] According to economist Robert Tatum, Leviticus instructs us that in a sinful world, some economic inequality is expected but we should still pay attention to factors that both worsen or ameliorate it.[10] Jubilee also suggests that the biblical God envisions wealth to be transferred through neighbour relations to rectify injustice. This makes the provision for equality within groups who are known to each other, as well as more widely. In other words, we should pay attention to inequalities within nations as well as between. It is important to remedy economic inequality even within countries like the UK that are wealthy in global terms.

Theologian Walter Brueggemann describes Jubilee as a radical teaching showing that the economy should be subordinate to the wellbeing of the whole community:

Social relationships between neighbours – creditors and debtors – are more important and definitional than the economic realities under consideration and there should be no permanent underclass in Israel, so that even the poor are assured wherewithal to participate in the economy.[11]

Jubilee is also demonstrative of the difference between inequalities of wealth and income. French economist Thomas Piketty, whose work has been central to the rise of the inequality paradigm, finds that the rate of return on wealth is greater than the rate of economic growth.[12] This means that inequalities of wealth are more pervasive, regardless of whether income levels are also unequal. Jubilee provides a means of routinely correcting for inequalities of wealth (specifically of land) separately from any intervention to equalise income through taxation and transfers.

It is unclear whether the principle of Jubilee was ever fully implemented, although some more recent historical evidence shows that Jubilee events did occur regularly in the ancient Middle East but Israel was unique in codifying this.[13] Regardless, this "makes it no less God's will for Old Testament times"[14] and Jubilee remains an indication of an envisioned society in which inequalities are addressed.[15]

While Jubilee was undoubtedly good news for the poor, it might not be so welcome for those who stood to lose their excess land when the shofar sounded to signal the Jubilee year. We might observe the same for the pursuit of a more egalitarian economy today. It is one of the reasons that cross-partisan, cross-demographic consensus on tackling inequality is hard to come by. (The mass reallocation of resources on the scale of Jubilee would evidently fail the "not packaged as redistribution" electoral test implied by the KCL data cited in our introduction.[16]) Of the policy solutions to remedy inequality, whether by taxation or transfer, most revolve around some form of sacrifice from those who are at present better off.

What is condemned?

Secondly, we consider **what is condemned** in the Bible. While legislation gives a sense of God's ideal, condemnation provides insight into what is simply unacceptable. Here, we turn from the legal texts to the insights of the Old Testament prophets. Like much of the Old Testament prophetic literature, the book of Amos is full of criticism for the wealthy who do not live justly. The prophet places an emphasis on pursuing economic justice, suggesting it is more important than ritual or worship if these are not accompanied by a just lifestyle.

> *Even though you bring me burnt offerings and grain offerings, I will not accept them... Away with the noise of your songs! I will not listen to the music of your harps. But let justice roll on like a river, righteousness like a never-failing stream! (Amos 5:22-24)*

Amos was writing at a time of significant economic change, with greater disparities emerging in Israel between the haves and have-nots. Wealth was becoming more concentrated in the hands of a few while the majority struggled for a subsistence income.[17] Archaeologists have suggested that the development of status differences manifested in physical property, and the associated social consequences, occurred around this time.[18] In short, houses were no longer all the same size.

Anthropologist James Woodburn demonstrated that the most egalitarian societies are those with immediate return economies.[19] That is, those where everything is eaten on the day it is collected or shared out among the community rather than being hoarded. In the injustices described by the prophets, we see how this form of economy is being dismantled and covetous behaviour is increasing. For example, Micah rails against those who "covet fields and seize them, and houses, and take them" (2:2), reiterating the notion that property was by then something coveted. Micah came after Amos chronologically, reiterating the unjust trajectory of the economy. Much like today, the prophets' excoriation of inequality comes as it was a burgeoning social problem.

Amos contrasts the unjust actions of the wealthy with the righteous living and ethical standards demanded by God of all. People groups are condemned for their exploitative behaviour, in the face of which they are told God will not relent. The cities of Gaza (1:6) and Tyre (1:9) are castigated for taking other communities captive and selling them for gain. The Ammonite nation faces condemnation for killing the women of Gilead "in order to extend his borders" (1:13). The motivation behind wealth accumulation is central to the condemnation, as is the ill treatment of others to which it leads. The means of gaining wealth as well as the hoarding of it are again viewed together in Amos 3:10, where the Lord declares that "they do not know how to do right who store up in their fortresses what they have plundered and looted".

Much of Amos's writing on inequality resonates today; he scathingly addresses the women who "oppress the poor and crush the needy" (4:1) while asking their husbands to bring them drinks. Rutledge reimagines this as "affluent women in fashionable sections of town who sit around their swimming pools... having their nails done and sipping cocktails high above the struggles of the poor."[20] This provides a vivid, relatable picture of the extravagance and indifference to injustice that the prophet was denouncing. The prophet's words are not just an ancient text, but one that speaks to issues manifest in every society, in every time.

God's condemnation of those who abide by the rituals of worship yet are indifferent to injustice is also clear. It is voiced as strongly as God "despising" religious festivals, which are "like a stench" (5:21) until justice and righteousness prevail (5:24). Rutledge calls this "one of the most striking passages in the prophetic literature," in which God "declares his opposition not only toward the rich but also toward good churchgoing people who are oblivious to inequity."[21] We should not assume this applies any less in our own context. The "denial" of justice to the oppressed (2:7) suggests that the people have the capacity to effect justice but choose not to.

What is modelled?

Finally, we can consider **what is modelled** by the historical texts, through the Old Testament narratives, the life of Jesus and the practices of the early church in the New Testament.

In Exodus, the Israelites are in the desert without food or water when God sends manna to sustain them. This practically demonstrates God's provision of enough and shows his economic principles.

> *Then the Lord said to Moses, "I will rain down bread from heaven for you. The people are to go out each day and gather enough for that day. In this way, I will test them and see whether they will follow my instructions. On the sixth day they are to*

prepare what they bring in, and that is to be twice as much as they gather on the other days." (Exodus 16:4-5)

The need for fair distribution of manna is emphasised, with those who have gathered more instructed to share with those who have gathered less so that each has only what they need (16:18). Sociologist and theologian Jacques Ellul wrote that the gathering of manna shows the value of enough; money should serve to meet only basic needs, with the rest distributed to meet others' needs. Ellul saw this as a "very clear indication that money, in the Christian life, is made in order to be given away" rather than endlessly accumulated.[22]

Although it is God's grace that ensures there is enough manna for everyone, there is still a human responsibility to distribute it well and with consideration for others.

The work of Nobel Prize-winning development economist Amartya Sen reinforces this in a secular context. Sen theorises that famines are the result of some people not having access to their entitlement of enough food, rather than because there was not enough food available.[23] This "entitlement failure", as he calls it, stems from a lack of democracy. In other words, it is a failure of human responsibility not of the earth; a spiritual rather than solely economic problem.

It is also stressed that manna cannot be hoarded; there are clear instructions only to collect enough for the day. When the Israelites respond to this by anxiously trying to store it regardless (v20), this proves futile. Brueggemann says this is because "bread given out of inexplicable divine generosity does not function according to [human] quotas of desire."[24] Whilst the human instinct is to accumulate, this goes against the responsibility to distribute justly. The earth and its resources have the potential to provide for all, including the poor, if they are not hoarded by the wealthiest.

Moving to the New Testament, throughout the gospels Jesus showed in both his life and his teaching that he was fundamentally more interested in the impact of economics on the relationships around him than economics itself.[26] He was demonstrably concerned with both spiritual and economic equality, overturning societal hierarchies in the way he befriended and valued those considered as outcasts (for example, eating with tax collectors and sinners in Matthew 9 and Luke 5).

In the Sermon on the Mount (Matthew 5-7), Jesus reverses typical understandings of what it means to be blessed, including the poor, the destitute and the rejected among those who are "blessed". His teaching on storing up treasure in heaven makes clear that we should not accumulate excess possessions in this life, nor is it possible to serve both God and material wealth. He also publicly declares the "year of the Lord's favour" (Luke 4:19), understood as the arrival of the Jubilee year and the accompanying equalisation and redistribution of resources.

Although never intended as "explicit discourses on economic theory,"[26] the parables Jesus told offer an understanding of inequality. Anglican bishop John Taylor noted that in the parable of the Prodigal Son, the prodigal "remembered his father's home as the place where even the lowest paid servant has enough and to spare" and sees this as an endorsement of the virtue of enough.[27] The parable of the Good Samaritan (Luke 10) is instructive on the universal responsibility to love our neighbour, as well as challenging societal preconceptions of status. For instance, it has been interpreted as a challenge to the caste system that entrenches deep socioeconomic inequalities in Indian society.[28]

The early church in Acts is another common reference point for a Christian economic vision. One particular passage describes the way of life that characterised the earliest Christian followers:

> *All the believers were together and had everything in common. They sold property and possessions to give to anyone who had need. (Acts 2:44-45).*

These verses come in the context of a close-knit, faithful community of believers, committed to each other and to the gospel. The strength of financial and social fellowship is stressed, with the fledgling church sometimes presented as a radical example of communalism. (Although subsequent verses indicate that they had their own homes, and thus that private property was not complete anathema.)

The Acts narrative does not state that all were substantively equal, but rather that "that there were no needy persons among them" (4:34) because of a radical ethic of sharing enacted through relationship. The close community typified by the early church moderated its own economic distribution and aspired to avoid extremes of wealth or poverty.

In terms of contemporary inequality, this points towards an approach of compassion and redistribution in order to tackle both material need and inequality. Again, the goal is not complete equality but rather the elimination of need through sharing. Generosity rather than selfishness and hoarding, "accompanied by compassionate commitment to doing what will most help the genuinely needy" remains a priority.[29] The value of enough is reiterated here in the way the early Christians shared with each other, in the same way that the Israelites redistributed manna.

1 Perfect, S., *Bridging the Gap: Economic Inequality and Church Responses in the UK* (London: Theos, 2020), p. 49.

2 Waterman, A., 'Inequality and Social Evil: Wilkinson and Pickett on The Spirit Level' *Faith & Economics 63*, (2014), p. 38.

3 Jubilee Debt Campaign, About Us. (2021). Available at: jubileedebt.org.uk/about-us

4 Foroohar, R., 'A student debt jubilee could kickstart US economic recovery'. *Financial Times,* (December 2020). Available at: www.ft.com/content/e309ed81-5949-4d46-909f-a4ff04ccd7b5

5 Mladin, N.,. '"Forgive us our debts": lending, borrowing, and debt forgiveness in Christian perspective' in *Financing Prosperity by Dealing with Debts*, eds. C. Harker and A. Horton, (London: UCL Press, forthcoming).

6 Sider, R., Rich *Christians in an Age of Hunger: Moving from Affluence to Generosity* (Nashville, TN: Thomas Nelson Publishers, 1978), p. 71.

7 Mills, P., 'The great financial crisis: a biblical diagnosis', *Jubilee Centre Cambridge Papers Vol 20:1*. (2011). Available at: www.jubilee-centre.org/cambridge-papers/the-great-financial-crisis-a-biblical-diagnosis-by-paul-mills

8 North, R., *Sociology of the Biblical Jubilee* (Rome: Pontifical Biblical Institute, 1954), p. 175.

9 Sider, R., *Rich Christians*, p. 72.

10 Tatum, R., 'Homo Economicus as Fallen Man: The Need for Theological Economics', *Journal of Markets & Morality*, Vol 20:1, (2017), p.132.

11 Brueggemann, W., *Truth Speaks to Power: The Countercultural Nature of Scripture* (Louisville, KY: Westminster John Knox Press, 2013), p. 123.

12 Piketty, T., *Capital in the Twenty-First Century*, Translated by A. Goldhammer. (Cambridge, MA: Harvard University Press, 2014).

13 Hudson, M., *...and forgive them their debts: Lending, Foreclosure and Redemption from Bronze Age to the Jubilee Year* (Dresden: ISLET-Verlag, 2018), p. xi.

14 Blomberg, C., *Neither Poverty nor Riches: A biblical theology of possessions* (Downers Grove, IL: InterVarsity Press, 1999), p.45.

15 Finn, D., *Christian Economic Ethics* (Minneapolis, MN: Fortress Press, 2013), p.62.

16 Duffy et al., *Unequal Britain*, p. 58.

17 Blomberg, C., *Neither Poverty nor Riches*, p.54.

18 Sider, R., *Rich Christians*, p. 45.

19 Woodburn, J., 'Egalitarian Societies', *Man*, Vol. 17, No. 3., (1982), pp. 431-451.

20 Rutledge, F., *The Crucifixion*, p.177.

21 Rutledge, F., *The Crucifixion,*, p.177.

22 Ellul, J., *Money and Power, ed. LaVonne Neff*. (Eugene, OR: Wipf and Stock Publishers, 2009 [1950]), p.52.

23 Sen, A., *Poverty and Famines: An Essay on Entitlement and Deprivation*. (Oxford: Oxford University Press, 1981).

24 Brueggemann, W., *Money and Possessions* (Louisville, KY: Westminster John Knox Press, 2016).

25 Perfect, S., *Bridging the Gap*, p. 45.

26 Blomberg, C., *Neither Poverty nor Riches*, p.112.

27 Taylor, J. (1975), *Enough is Enough* (London: SCM Press, 1975).

28 Gnanavaram, M., '"Dalit Theology" and the Parable of the Good Samaritan'. *Journal for the Study of the New Testament Vol 15:50*, (1993), pp. 59-83.

29 Blomberg, C., *Neither Poverty nor Riches*, p.175.

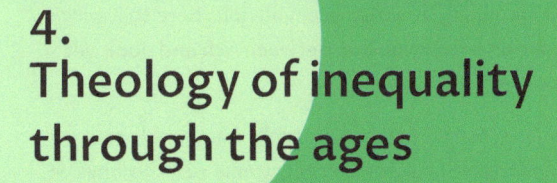

4.
Theology of inequality through the ages

Economic inequality has long existed, rising and falling idiosyncratically over time. However, it is relatively recently that we have begun to name it as such, whether as a theological concern or a socioeconomic concept. For example, Ron Sider's book Rich Christians in an Age of Hunger was groundbreaking when it was first published in 1978, but is notable now for the way it seems to skirt around the subject of inequality without naming it.[1] It begins with some stark statistics about global poverty before addressing what this means for a wealthy Christian audience in the West. To a reader familiar with the modern focus on inequality, it would seem obvious here to explore the inegalitarian relationship between rich and poor, yet Sider does not.

Similarly, Martin Luther King spoke frequently about the uncomfortable juxtaposition of extreme wealth alongside extreme poverty, but did not name this as inequality. In his famous 'I Have a Dream' speech in 1963, he stated that "as long as there is poverty in this world, no man can be totally rich even if he has a billion dollars"[2], implicitly identifying inequality as an obstacle to human flourishing for both rich and poor. In another sermon, he outlined the way that such inequality was contrary to God's will because "God never intended for one group of people to live in superfluous inordinate wealth, while others live in abject deadening poverty."[3]

In this section, we explore what several key theological texts from throughout Christian history say about inequality, whether or not they use the word explicitly.

Church Fathers

Were it written today, John Chrysostom's fourth-century discourse *On Wealth and Poverty* might be titled *On Inequality*. It deals less with the two concepts independently and more with their coexistence and the inequitable relationship between them. Chrysostom takes the parable of Lazarus and the rich man in Luke 16 as his text.[4] This is a story told by Jesus about a rich man who lived a life of luxury while ignoring a poor man (Lazarus) who sat outside his gates hoping for charity. When both men die, Lazarus goes to heaven while the rich man is condemned to hell.

Chrysostom's exegesis of the passage may have been directed at his fourth-century congregation, but the denunciation of the abuse of wealth and property, and its consequences for the lives of the poor, has a strong contemporary resonance too.

Chrysostom begins by saying that the rich man is chastised not only for his life of luxury, but also specifically for how he lived wickedly in such close proximity to the poor man. The rich man lived comfortably, without experiencing any of the "ills of human life" but felt no pity or compassion for Lazarus. The poor man was situated outside the rich man's house, where he could not be ignorant of him, which according to Chrysostom indicates he might express even greater callousness to those suffering further away. Our position in the scale of the economy is thus seen to affect our moral obligations and the way God views our actions:

> *It is not the same thing for one living in poverty not to assist those who are in need, as for one who enjoys such luxury to neglect others who are wasting away through hunger.*[5]

He draws on the idea that all things ultimately belong to the Lord, echoing Jesus' words in Luke 3:11 in suggesting that to keep excess wealth or possessions for oneself is tantamount to theft.[6]

> *The rich are in possession of things that belong to the poor, even if their property be gained justly or by inheritance; in fact, from whatsoever their substance be derived.*[7]

Inequality occurs in part as a consequence of decisions about the distribution of material goods. However if everything is the Lord's, Chrysostom says, we have no right to make inequitable choices. He equates unfair distribution of the things we have received with the actions of a corrupt tax collector who does not distribute taxes as ordered by the king:

> *If you have received more than others, you have received it not that you only should spend it, but that you should be a good steward of it for the advantage of others.*[8]

As in this particular passage, Chrysostom uses the word 'receive' as opposed to 'have' or 'possess' consistently in reference to material goods, stressing that, like the Israelites' manna, they are temporary blessings given by God rather than earned.

Chrysostom refers several times to justice in the afterlife and the idea of death as the great leveller in which there is complete equality. None is exempt from the ultimate judgment, least of all the rich:

> *When all is ashes, all cinders and dust, all is lamentation and mourning... then was made manifest the real power of gold and of all the rest of his wealth.*[9]

Chrysostom makes clear that his congregation should see themselves in the position of the rich man not Lazarus, and respond accordingly in pursuing justice. The words addressed to the rich man in the next life, he says, are intended to shake their hearers into avoiding the same fate. This should also shape the response of contemporary listeners hearing these words in the knowledge of the inequality that exists in our own society.

Also writing in the fourth century, St Ambrose is scathing in his analysis of the effects of wealth on human behaviour. He takes the story of Naboth and Ahab in 1 Kings 21 as evidence of this.[10] Ahab is already wealthy but covets Naboth's vineyard for the purpose of increasing his own wealth. When Naboth will not sell the vineyard, Ahab goes into mourning – a visceral reaction to his greed not being satisfied and the poor not being swayed by his power. His desire for greater wealth escalates further and leads him to behave corruptly against Naboth.

For Ambrose, this story is emblematic of human nature. There is not just one singular Ahab and one Naboth, he says, but an endemic cycle of greed and exploitation in which we all encounter both Ahab and Naboth as economic actors.

> *It is not one Ahab who was born, therefore, but – what is worse – Ahab is born every day, and never does he die as far as this world is concerned. For each one who dies there are many others who rise up; there are more who steal property than who lose it. It is not one poor man, Naboth, who was slain; every day Naboth is struck down, every day the poor man is slain.*[11]

The link between wealth and greed is evident; one feeds the other and fuels inequalities of economics and power. Taken to its extreme, covetousness changes how we see other humans, is destructive of human dignity and removes our ability to see the face of God in others.[12]

Ambrose echoes Chrysostom's emphasis on the temporariness of wealth, which cannot last beyond the grave. Birth and death alike do not discriminate, applying equally to rich and poor. Dead bodies wrapped in expensive cloth are "losses to the living and of no help to the dead."[13] Here he also highlights the generational impact of wealth and inheritance, reinforcing bad economic habits, leading to greater inequality and causing arguments among families.

In a passage that feels remarkably contemporary, Ambrose rails against the rich who abstract themselves from the human consequences of their economic practices. He states that if people die or suffer elsewhere in the production chain, the rich are not absolved from responsibility. Reading this in the light of the injustices perpetuated by the gig economy, fast fashion's reliance on sweatshops, and poor industrial working conditions is sobering.

> *How many die so that pleasures may be prepared for you! Deadly is your greed, deadly your luxury. One man tumbled from a rooftop when he was readying large storerooms for your grain. Another fell from the top of a tall tree while searching for the sorts of grapes to bring down for the proper wines to be served at your banqueting.*[14]

Ambrose expounds not only the physical consequences of this, but also the emotional toll of injustice on the poor. Again, this is a reminder to those who appear to be on the 'right' end of the economic spectrum that their behaviour is not without consequence for their neighbours.

This highlights a key moral distinction between poverty and inequality, whereby economic inequality implicates all of us. It is by its nature a relational problem. To speak about poverty allows us to be concerned but abstracted from the issue if we ourselves are not considered 'the poor'.

To speak about inequality forces us each instead to examine our own economic privilege and position in relation to others. **There are compelling theological reasons why the rich and indeed the 'middling' should care about inequality, not just out of pity for the poor but out of concern for themselves and their own spiritual health.** The rich man's covetousness, according to Ambrose, is more spiritually damaging to his soul than the poor man's hunger.

Modern voices

If the Church Fathers like Ambrose and Chrysostom have much to say about inequality, so too do their more recent counterparts. Catholic Social Teaching (CST), expressed through papal encyclicals, makes a notable contribution to our theological understanding of the topic. Although Pope Leo XIII's 1891 encyclical *Rerum Novarum* uses the word "inequalities" only once as a passing reference to differences in status, it is a seminal text in CST with clear relevance here.[15]

The title means "of revolutionary change" yet it cuts a path between left and right-wing economics, eschewing both capitalism and communism. Leo XIII recognises that rising support for socialist ideologies at the time was driven by the unequal distribution of resources within the market, but sees socialism as the wrong solution to a genuine problem.

> *The hiring of labour and the conduct of trade are concentrated in the hands of comparatively few; so that a small*

> *number of very rich men have been able to lay upon the teeming masses of the labouring poor a yoke little better than that of slavery itself.*[16]

The encyclical restates the Catholic Church's defence of the right to private property and as such is excused from accusations of socialist bias. It asserts that abolishing private property would harm workers and distort the role of the state, depriving individuals of the capacity for self-improvement.

Leo XIII quotes St Thomas Aquinas, who wrote that it is both lawful and necessary for people to hold private property. However, in the same breath, the pope warns against unrestricted capitalism. Private ownership is in accordance with the law of nature, but carries a responsibility to the common good, rather than absolute freedom of use:

> Whoever has received from the divine bounty a large share of temporal blessings, whether they be external and material, or gifts of the mind, has received them for the purpose of using them for the perfecting of his own nature, and, at the same time, that he may employ them, as the steward of God's providence, for the benefit of others.[17]

This passage echoes Chrysostom's insistence on seeing material goods as temporal blessings to be held lightly rather than possessions to be accumulated. Again, it frames anything we 'possess' as something we have "received" rather than 'earned'. The notion of stewardship also recalls the environmental responsibility we have to the planet.

Rerum Novarum also speaks to the necessity of universal access to the basic essentials required for a good life. We might see it as emphasising the need to bring everyone within the inner ring (or floor) of the doughnut model (see p.8), while at the same time cautioning against the unfettered capitalism that extends consumption beyond the outer ring.

Fair wages for workers, Leo XIII suggests, must be generous enough to support a whole family, with enough left for the worker to improve their condition over time. In our roundtables, we heard that inequality is particularly concerning when it is so intractable that individuals are incapable of escaping its effects. Too great a level of poverty, or too wide an inequality gap, makes this harder.

The provision made here for potential economic mobility, beyond subsistence, is therefore important, but so is the fact that it is made the responsibility of the employer not only the employee. It is not solely a matter of the worker's good stewardship or ability to "lift themselves up", but also the duty of the employer to treat their workers well enough that they have the means to do so. The trade union movement is positioned as important in this. According to Leo XIII, this will not only improve the material conditions of working people, but will also reduce the social inequalities that develop as a result of economic disparities.

> *If working people can be encouraged to look forward to obtaining a share in the land, the consequence will be that the gulf between vast wealth and sheer poverty will be bridged over, and the respective classes will be brought nearer to one another.*[18]

In Rerum Novarum, Leo XIII articulated what would later become the principle of the "preferential option for the poor", central to both CST and the liberation theology movement. Starting from the acknowledgment that "God Himself seems to incline rather to those who suffer misfortune", this underlines the dignity of the poor and argues that preference should be shown to the wellbeing of the least well off.[19] Whilst this appears to be concerned with addressing poverty rather than inequality, it sets a precedent that our economic and moral decisions should not be neutral.

This papal teaching finds a secular counterpart in the ethics of "prioritarianism", which argues that incremental increases in wellbeing are morally more valuable the lower the start point, rather than because of the size of the increment.[20] In other words, it is morally better to improve the lives of the least well-off, showing preference to the poor. In an age of climate crisis driven by overconsumption, however, we might argue that this has lost currency. The focus on poverty is no longer enough when the excesses of the rich must also be restrained. If the bias to the poor instructs us to care for those who fall beneath the floor of the doughnut model, now is also the time to consider what it might mean to address those living above its ceiling.

More recently, Pope Francis' encyclical *Fratelli Tutti*, published in 2020 during the Covid-19 pandemic, demonstrates the increased contemporary interest of the Church in the topic, explicitly referring to inequality as one of the trends in the world "that hinder[s] the development of universal fraternity".[21]

Francis says that the "reductive anthropological vision" of the prevailing global economic model has led to a reduced collective identity, diminishing our sense of human belonging and causing deep disillusionment.[22] This has strengthened the interests of the most powerful, and left poorer groups even more vulnerable. The economic system has proved effective for growth but less so for integral human development, with wealth and inequality increasing in tandem and new forms of poverty emerging. This growing gulf is true both between and within regions and countries.

Francis cites various early theologians, including Chrysostom and St Gregory the Great, who articulated the idea that what we have is to be shared and that excess wealth is theft.

As a community, we have an obligation to ensure that every person lives with dignity and has sufficient opportunities for his or her integral development. If one person lacks what is necessary to live with dignity, it is because another person is detaining it.[23]

In this conception of the social role of property, excessive economic inequality becomes systematised theft when it prevents all members of the community from living with basic dignity.

Key to Francis's approach is the sense that material inequality is not itself the only thing that matters. The right to human dignity is universal and this should not be based on productivity or capacity, or fraternity and solidarity will be compromised. Francis quotes his own earlier magisterial document discussing inequalities of birth, recognising that some are born into greater economic stability and with education and health care guaranteed, whereas many others are not. However, this must not translate into parallel inequalities of dignity:

The mere fact that some people are born in places with fewer resources or less development does not justify the fact that they are living with less dignity.[24]

Fratelli Tutti makes it clear that the responsibility for resolving social problems like excessive economic inequality does not lie solely with the state. As human beings and as Christians, Francis says, we are each accountable for transforming the parts of society that do not currently serve collective flourishing. There is a need for fundamental change to heal the grave structural deficiencies in global society, and we are all implicated in working towards that:

> *We should not expect everything from those who govern us, for that would be childish. We have the space we need for co-responsibility in creating and putting into place new processes and changes. Let us take an active part in renewing and supporting our troubled societies.*[25]

We are compelled by what Francis calls "social love'" to work towards better forms of economic developments, new ideas and transformative structures, at both a micro- and macro-level.

> *It is an act of charity to assist someone suffering, but it is also an act of charity, even if we do not know that person, to work to change the social conditions that caused his or her suffering.*[26]

Policy-making can be an expression of this social love, if it pursues the common good and humanity of all. Francis notes that the pandemic has highlighted how connected we are globally and the ensuing responsibility we have to our global neighbours. Inequality matters at a global scale, as well as within each country, and we cannot be indifferent to that.

1 Sider, R., *Rich Christians*.

2 King, M. L., *I Have a Dream* (1963) Speech delivered at the March on Washington for Jobs and Freedom, Washington, D.C. Transcript available at: www.npr.org/2010/01/18/122701268/i-have-a-dream-speech-in-its-entirety?t=1631283255014

3 King, M. L., *Paul's Letter to American Christians* (1956) Speech delivered at Dexter Avenue Baptist Church, Montgomery, Alabama. Transcript available at: kinginstitute.stanford.edu/king-papers/publications/knock-midnight-inspiration-great-sermons-reverend-martin-luther-king-jr-1

4 St John Chrysostom, *On Wealth and Poverty* (Crestwood, New York: St Vladimir's Seminary Press, 1984)

5 Chrysostom, discourse 1.

6 Numerous other theologians, including Dorothy Day, Basil the Great and St Oscar Romero, have used this same analogy and are widely quoted as such.

7 Chrysostom, discourse II.

8 Ibid.

9 Ibid.

10 Ambrose, *On Naboth*. Available online at: www.hymnsandchants.com/Texts/Sermons/Ambrose/OnNaboth.htm

11 Ambrose, *On Naboth*, § 1.1.

12 Perfect, S. , *Bridging the Gap*, p. 6.

13 Ambrose, *On Naboth*, § 1.3.

14 Ambrose, *On Naboth*, § 5.20.

15 Pope Leo XIII, *Rerum Novarum: Encyclical Letter of Pope Leo Xiii on Capital and Labour* (1891). Available at: www.vatican.va/content/leo-xiii/en/encyclicals/documents/hf_l-xiii_enc_15051891_rerum-novarum.html

16 *Rerum Novarum*, § 7.

17 *Rerum Novarum*, § 22.

18 *Rerum Novarum*, § 47.

19 Rerum Novarum, section 24.

20 Temkin, L., 'Equality, Priority, and the Levelling-Down Objection' in Clayton, M. & Williams, A. (eds.), *The Ideal of Equality (London: Macmillan*, 2000), pp. 126-61.

21 Pope Francis, *Fratelli Tutti* (2020). Available at: www.vatican.va/content/francesco/en/encyclicals/documents/papa-francesco_20201003_enciclica-fratelli-tutti.html, § 9.

22 *Fratelli Tutti*, § 22.

23 *Fratelli Tutti*, § 118.

24 *Fratelli Tutti*, § 106.

25 *Fratelli Tutti*, § 77.

26 *Fratelli Tutti*, § 186.

5
Policy implications and recommendations

We concluded from our roundtables that social and relational harms are among the most important criteria by which inequality can be deemed to be excessive. However, reaching a shared position on *solutions* to excessive inequality between left- and right-wing perspectives is trickier, because it may require commitment to policies that are typically seen as the preserve of one group or another.

That acknowledged, theology, with its well-developed understanding of how to organise human relationships in balance with one another and the wider natural world, has much to offer here.

In this final chapter, we consider potential policy solutions to inequality, in light of the theological principles explored thus far. This is not intended as an exhaustive or prescriptive programme for addressing inequality, but rather focuses on ideas that can reach across political divides and draw consensus. The hope is that policymakers and church leaders alike might be inspired to see that **theology can offer "a vision of how the economy could be recalibrated from one of exclusion and self-interest to one of hope"**.[1]

As Jonathan Haidt notes about the consensus-driven research on child poverty that inspired our work, it is "hard to get people to agree to violate their sacred values," and yet this is assumed to be what it takes to achieve a cross-partisan policy platform. Haidt cites the following example: "we got the people on the left to actually agree that marriage is actually... really important for understanding poverty and inequality, and we got the right to actually agree to recommend birth control."[2] He points out that often when people think they are being asked to violate something sacred, they may simply be talking at cross-purposes about different valuable concepts.

Solutions to the challenge of excessive economic inequality can be both micro- or macro-level responses, ranging from state interventions, better business practices or (even non-economic) community initiatives to rethinking our entire economic model. The role of the state in mediating the economy, and the balance between predistribution and redistribution, is a sticking point in conversations around economic inequality. Different conceptions of the role of the state and the importance of individual and market freedom underlie tensions between different positions.

> **When people think they are being asked to violate something sacred, they may simply be talking at cross-purposes about different valuable concepts.**

Our consensus process has demonstrated, however, that the relational dimension of inequality is where agreement is most easily found, and the 'human meaning of inequality' is a more unanimous cause for concern that the economic aspects. In proposing solutions, therefore, we begin with non-economic solutions aimed at improving social bonds across different groups within our communities, before considering economic policy initiatives involving business and the state.

Relational solutions

Extreme inequality is not a solely economic problem, and neither therefore are the measures of addressing its social consequences solely economic. Some of these policies might still involve the state, but in areas other than fiscal policy. Together, **they reorient our social interactions and relationships towards a more egalitarian way of being.**

First, we need to find more opportunities for a genuinely common life within society. As Jon Yates argues in his book *Fractured*, people tend towards those like them when given the choice, choosing to divide rather than unite across demographic groups.[3] Yates calls this impulse 'People Like Me syndrome' and it serves to entrench socioeconomic divides and inequalities. It is therefore crucial to combat if we are to tackle inequality; the tendency for division along social lines may undermine even the strongest economic measures of distribution and egalitarianism.

The education system is one place in which this impulse becomes especially apparent, with unequal social relationships emerging even among young people. Yates suggests that a National Citizen Scheme for secondary school age pupils might combat this, but ought to be designed so that young people do not decide the groups in which they are placed.[4] Similar opportunities for organised mixing and equal risks of segregation will emerge at other points in life too, whether in the workplace, parenthood and childcare, or retirement. Efforts to bring different groups together at all of these stages, as well as encouraging intergenerational cohesion, would be equally beneficial. As previous Theos research has found, faith groups and places of worship can be prime examples of this, as spaces that naturally bring together people across different socioeconomic backgrounds and age groups.[5]

The issue of private education is somewhat contentious here. While there are advocates for its complete abolition, this is not a consensus-winning proposal. Private schools are already required by law to demonstrate their public benefit credentials in order to maintain charitable status. This can take the form of partnerships with local state schools, or the provision of scholarships for disadvantaged pupils.[6]

These measures focus on greater equality of access to a good education, but could go further in building relationships within local communities.[7] Private schools might start to see themselves as anchor institutions, engaging genuinely with local residents.

Infrastructure also has a role to play. The geographical inequalities between regions that require 'levelling up' are also present within towns and cities. The phenomenon of 'poor doors' – segregated entrances of housing developments for different categories of residents – is an example of this, entrenching inequalities of wealth and income and shaping social relations in communities. The same is true of developments where social housing is entirely separate from privately owned housing. A survey in 2018 found that less than half (41%) of people in England would feel comfortable living next to social housing and almost a quarter (24%) would be actively uncomfortable, which emphasises how inequalities have social as well as economic manifestations.[8]

In addition to housing, **shared public spaces** can engender more equal relationships within communities. In 2019, it was reported that a housing development in Central London had prohibited the children of its social tenants from accessing communal play areas, although they later changed this policy after complaints.[9] One in five Londoners, and one in eight people nationally, have no access to a private garden and so parks and other communal outdoor spaces provide a valued resource for wellbeing and mixing across social boundaries.[10] This has been particularly apparent during the pandemic. Town planning that encourages universal communal space can lead to greater wellbeing as well as more cohesive and egalitarian community relationships.

In the roundtables, we noted that the role of marriage and **stable household relationships** is often ignored in discussions of economic inequality. There are some recognised links between family structures and poverty, and the role this plays in both poverty and inequality is significant.

For example, married families are less likely to be in poverty than single parent households.[11] There is evidence that family structure has an impact on educational outcomes, with some studies suggesting that children in single parent families fare worse in literacy and numeracy tests. There are demonstrable differences in outcomes for children born to single-parent households versus married or cohabiting, even once the associated economic disadvantage is accounted for.[12]

Family breakdown is also associated with homelessness, with 49% of young homeless people giving this as the reason.[13]

None of these figures alone prove causation but they do underline that relational stability is a significant aspect of financial stability. Policy initiatives that support stable households are therefore likely to reduce economic inequality too, albeit indirectly, not least because of the improved health and educational outcomes associated with it. Examples of this might include better early years support to support new parents. Other measures to support family life might include greater transferable tax allowances or relationship support provision.

What can the market do?

As well as relational interventions, we also contend that business practices can play a role in reducing inequities in the economy. One way in which business might do this would be through the voluntary restriction of executive pay and the setting of **pay ratios between employees**.

In 2019, the highest paid FTSE-100 CEO received a total pay package equivalent to 1,935 times the median salary of a full-time UK worker, with the median FTSE-100 CEO earning 119 times the median salary. Within individual companies, the average ratio of the highest and lowest paid employees was 84:1, and this ratio is growing.[14] Salary inequality of this form is getting worse, making regulatory measures more pressing. Choosing to limit this ratio to a smaller level would reduce inequality within organisations and thus within society more broadly.

The ratio set could be large enough to allow different roles and responsibilities to be paid accordingly and this intervention does not seek to eradicate all inequality. Neither does it set a specific minimum/maximum wage arbitrarily, which some would consider too much external intervention. Instead, the highest paid employee's pay is directly tied to that of the lowest paid. If a CEO seeks an inordinately high pay package for themselves, they can do so only by increasing the pay of their least senior members of staff accordingly.

The idea of a pay ratio stacks up favourably against the theological importance of relationship and human flourishing established in our research. In economic terms, it hangs on the connection between employees or individuals within a given organisation or group, and in social terms, it mediates the damaging power dynamics that can emerge with extremely hierarchical pay structures. The socio-psychological impact is also significant. The distrust and resentment that can emerge with greater financial inequality is harmful for human relationships, but a ratio underlines instead the connectedness of individuals within a community or company.

Reorienting our economy towards co-operative models (many of which are widely tried and tested) **and worker-led democracy** would also serve as a mechanism for predistribution that does not rely on the state. The co-operative business model again hinges on human relationships as the starting point for its economic vision of worker ownership and shared values. One of the largest and most successful co-operative enterprises in the world is the Mondragon Corporation in the Basque Country. It was founded by Father José Maria Arizmendiarrieta, a Catholic priest who recognised the need to create good employment as well as providing spiritual care in his small rural community in the aftermath of the Spanish Civil War. Fr Arizmendiarrieta's approach to economic development is summed up in his statement that "all economic, political and social problems are, in the final analysis, human problems."[15] This also sums up the basis for consensus in our roundtables.

The example of Mondragon demonstrates that an enterprise whose primary motivating factor is solidarity rather than profit does not have to be unprofitable. Today, it is a global federation of over 120 co-operatives with 75,000 member-employees. It is a successful business by any standard, with an annual turnover that makes one of the largest enterprises in Spain. It achieved this success through a humanistic vision of business yet without deprioritising economic growth completely. The company's mantra is 'humanity at work' and it is an enduring manifestation of the principles of solidarity and justice that are central to the Catholic Social Teaching espoused by its founder. Pay ratios within Mondragon do not exceed 9:1 and in most cases are closer to 5:1.

The co-operative model has had a transformative impact on the entire town of Mondragón and beyond. Because of the high proportion of local residents who work in the co-operative, there is a minimal degree of socioeconomic differentiation and low levels of poverty. The narrow pay ratio is effectively replicated across the whole community. Residents feel that the values of solidarity and democracy are firmly embedded in community identity and culture beyond the workplace.[16]

For Mondragon, the egalitarian model of cooperativism was central right from its beginnings, but it is possible to tweak existing business practices along similar lines to address inequality. However, by its nature, introducing a co-operative model has to be done collaboratively rather than legislated for or prescribed as a top-down approach, although tax breaks for companies adopting this model could be used as a means of incentivising it, for example.

What can the state do?

As previously alluded to, the role of the state in mediating inequality is a point of contention. The case for predistribution implies that the state has a role in preventing inequalities through ensuring a fairer initial distribution of resources, in addition to implementing taxation and welfare provision to correct for inequalities.[17] However, this requires a level of state intervention in the market with which not everyone is comfortable.

At the same time, **people are not merely economic equations to be fixed or inequalities to be levelled**

up, but potential to be developed, and economic policy solutions should reflect that. Within this, there is a place for redistributive taxation, but also for questioning the barriers that prevent people reaching their economic potential. Some roundtable participants framed this in terms of tackling inequality by empowering people to 'lift themselves' up or improve their own circumstances.

> **People are not merely economic equations to be fixed or inequalities to be levelled up, but potential to be developed.**

Policy proposals around this might include a **greater emphasis on adult education**. In the UK, 16% of the adult population are considered "functionally illiterate" according to data from the National Literacy Trust.[18] This is demonstrably a barrier to earning a wage and providing benefits to these individuals does little to address this. A generous or equitable benefit system alone cannot address these underlying educational challenges; as David Goodhart has noted, a more fundamental problem is that the British labour market is increasingly set up (economically and in terms of social status) to favour graduates, with decreased focus on, and funding for, other forms of training and education.[19] Funding for adult training fell by almost 15 per cent per worker in 2005-2011 and funding for continued vocational training recorded a cut of almost 30 per cent over the same time[20].

Increased investment in adult education and vocational training could therefore redress the challenges of educational inequalities, creating a system in which there are many routes to (many kinds of) success, and nobody is left behind forever because of their educational outcomes as a child.

Policy implications and recommendations

There is also a case to be made that redistributing money without investing in services to tackle the causes is a false economy. For example, there are over half a million dependent drinkers in the UK, but only 18% of these are receiving adequate treatment.[21] Nearly half (47%) of those in treatment live in the most deprived areas. However, paradoxically, nearly 60% of local authority areas have cut funding to addiction support services.[22] Similar arguments can be also be made about problem gambling, which affects almost 300,000 people in the UK, with equivalent shortfalls in recovery services.[23] Without holistic consideration of some of the causes of inequality, state redistribution might appear to rebalance the economic equation – but will only scratch the surface of the problem.

One radical model for this redistribution is universal basic services, which does not involve direct financial transfers. This is a form of social security in which all residents of a particular community or nation receive unconditional access to free basic public services provided centrally, whether that is travel, education, healthcare or other services.[24]

The range of services prioritised within this model is flexible and allows countries or regions to be responsive to which particular universal services would most benefit their citizens. In the UK, the NHS is a prime example of universal state provision of health care, which extends to free prescription medication in Wales and Scotland, but examples from around the world demonstrate this same principle. A growing number of cities and regions provide free Wi-Fi within their infrastructure, correcting for digital inequalities in the population. In 2020, Luxembourg introduced free nationwide public transport for citizens and visitors alike, with the government stating that "mobility is one of the most important challenges of humanity in the twenty-first century".[25]

Pope Francis writes in *Fratelli Tutti* that our response to poverty should recognise the specific resources by which it is manifested. By extension, we should also consider inequality of access to these resources, not only of income:

> *In other times, for example, lack of access to electric energy was not considered a sign of poverty, nor was it a source of hardship. Poverty must always be understood and gauged in the context of the actual opportunities available in each concrete historical period.*[26]

In each of these cases, the government or municipality in question have made decisions based on what would improve the specific wellbeing and life chances of their citizens and thus reduce inequities of access to the basics of life and flourishing. This is an indirect means of redistributing wealth, with a disproportionate benefit for those in low-income groups, gearing the economy to serve the weakest as part of the whole. It also equips all to improve their own life circumstances, an important test for proposals to meet if they are to draw consensus from the right as we have seen.

Redistribution within the **welfare system through transfers** is another part of the conversation. It was noted in the roundtables that the introduction of the furlough scheme in the UK during the pandemic has begun to change our collective mind-set about income. The scale of the economic challenges posed by the pandemic has meant that a wider section of the population has had recourse to the welfare system than is typically the case. It may be that individuals previously averse to the idea of non-means-tested benefits have a greater sympathy for these proposals as a result. It was suggested that if the grace of God is unconditional and generous, and this is the heart of the Christian faith, then the best gift we can offer society is to mirror that in our welfare provision.

An existing example of non-means-tested benefit highlighted by roundtable participants was that of **the UK child benefit system**, in which a set amount is paid to the parent or carer of every child regardless of their income, with taxation then recouping it from those earning over a threshold. This ensures every household has a basic minimum to provide for the children in it. Whether motivated by bureaucracy, ideology, or both, non-means-testing assumes that it is better to pay someone supposedly 'undeserving' i.e. who already earns 'too much' than to miss out paying someone on a lower income who needs the support. The equalising power dynamic of universality is in contrast with the power-from-above dynamic of means testing. This model therefore begins to address social inequalities as well as the economic ones.

Another variation of universal basic provision to achieve greater equality is the creation of a **universal basic capital grant**. This proposes that every citizen receives a grant of capital at a certain point. (The Child Trust Fund implemented between 2003 and 2010 was an example of this.)

Public policy expert Julian Le Grand proposes a £10,000 grant to every individual on his or her eighteenth birthday.[27] This grant would be financed out of general revenues and would reduce inequalities of wealth and opportunity, especially along ethnic lines. It would give all individuals access to a "trust fund" with which to "better themselves", whether through education or entrepreneurship, which is usually something only the wealthiest can rely upon. Le

Grand formulates how this could be paid for by an enhanced inheritance tax, thereby correcting for large generational inequalities too and using the accumulated wealth of one generation to stimulate the growth of the next. Like Jubilee, this would reset injustice by redistributing wealth between generations.

A further intervention discussed by roundtable participants was the creation of a **sovereign wealth fund or social wealth fund**, which could be used to fund this universal capital grant. This refers to a state-owned investment fund, which mobilises the financial value of public assets and uses the revenues to benefit citizens.[28] Existing examples of this use the assets of natural resources to invest in collective wealth building, similar to Old Testament treatment of the land as a basic, common asset that guarantees individuals' share in social and economic life.

Another possible formulation of the sovereign wealth fund involves the transfer of land, whether undeveloped or brownfield, as a state asset into such a fund.[29] Managing public assets in this way has the potential to generate public revenues which, properly shared, can begin to address inequality either through funding interventions which do so or directly through shared public dividends. The state of Alaska opts for the latter of these, paying an annual dividend to each citizen from its sovereign wealth fund based on the state's natural minerals, which are seen as the property of all. In 2015, this amounted to around £1500 per citizen.[30]

The local incarnation of these funds is community wealth funds, which draw on a localised asset base to boost the economy of a region and its residents. This keeps local wealth in the local area, with the potential to redistribute it creatively.

A local authority pension fund might be structured so as to benefit the local economy. In the North East of England, a shale wealth fund already exists to support communities near shale gas extraction sites.[31]

Whilst natural resources may not now be a sustainable form of this fund for the UK, Conservative peer Lord Wei has argued that a sovereign wealth fund based on entrepreneurship, research and development would increase the resilience of national finances.[32]

All this said, whilst the market and the welfare state can reduce inequalities to a point, it can never eradicate the need for some form of taxation – and indeed, very few people would argue for zero taxation, just as we have seen very few argue for complete economic equality. Greater predistribution can never completely eradicate the need for some taxation; the question, then, is how much. Taxation itself reinforces the social dynamic of the economy (what we owe to one another), as well as the theological principle that wealth is temporary and should be held lightly. It is therefore an appropriate means of ensuring that our best instincts are honoured, and these deep social obligations are met.

With this in mind, one way that effective taxation can reduce inequality is by prioritising the **elimination of tax havens**. These are enabled by the inability of the international community to agree to close loopholes that allow foreign investors to benefit from low levels of taxation. When the G7 recently agreed a historic global agreement on tax abuses by multinational companies, the UK government instantly pushed for the City of London to be exempt.[33] Revelations known as the Pandora Papers, which emerged as this research reached completion, highlighted the extent of offshore finance among the wealthy and powerful.[34]

This is a consequence of globalisation, whereby the financial system has expanded beyond the confines of a shared societal life and capital is infinitely mobile. We might suggest this is what happens when globalisation leads us to forget neighbourliness; when we become global without retaining the sense in which we still owe something to one another. In theological terms, tax havens are the result of a failure to love our global neighbours. A concerted effort to reduce this would increase tax revenues within countries, without affecting the majority of the population. Similarly, a clamp down on tax evasion and avoidance would increase taxation revenue streams without imposing any policy changes or new forms of taxation on the general population.

The gap between the richest and poorest households in the UK has also grown since the Covid-19 pandemic began.[35] The idea of a wealth tax has typically been a contentious policy debate, but we heard in the roundtables a greater sense of openness to this in light of the pandemic. While the pandemic has been a shared experience, its economic effects have been felt radically differently at various points in the income distribution. Some of the usual notions of personal responsibility or self-improvement do not necessarily apply to wealth earned during the pandemic, nor do the typical arguments against a wealth tax.

New ways of thinking about the economy

In our current economic paradigm, it seems there is no such thing as too much growth – no concept of **having 'enough'** – and what growth there is, is unevenly distributed. This is at the root of economic inequality. In addition to specific policy interventions, therefore, we suggest that a more fundamental paradigm shift is required in order to address economic inequality comprehensively. As theologian Kathryn Tanner writes, "without significant changes in the way money is made... religious calls for personal reformation do not go far enough in addressing the economic problems we face" – and to this, we might add the burgeoning environmental problems coming ever clearer into view.[36]

Agreement is further complicated by the varying importance placed on economic growth. It can be too easy to write off an opposing view or ascribe a particular –ism to it; for example, dismissing a perspective that prioritises economic growth as overly neoliberal, or the reverse as naively socialist. Motives for prioritising growth are more nuanced than sometimes presented; it can equally be pursued out of greed or as a means of poverty reduction.

Various roundtable participants rejected the notion of deprioritising economic growth altogether, but felt that such growth should be seen as a means rather than an end in itself. The framing of policies is therefore as important here as the content proposed. As discussed in the introductory chapters, it is essential to get beyond stereotypes in order to achieve transformation, but it is in discussing specific policies rather than broad-brush theories that these caricatures emerge.

We suggest that a Christian approach to inequality would mean **recalibrating the economy to prioritise wellbeing**, while recognising the appropriate role for growth in a healthy economy. In their book *The Economics of Arrival*, Jeremy Williams and Katherine Trebeck explore this possibility from a secular perspective, urging us to move from enlarging the economy to improving it, and outlining the benefits this would bring for all.[37] They suggest that economic growth is a journey towards a destination, an endpoint they call Arrival (in uppercase) or economic maturity. This frees us up to think about inequality slightly differently; when there is Enough, we can shift from quantity to quality and from accumulation to inclusion as economic policy priorities.

The GDP measures currently used as indicators of economic prosperity are a blunt instrument when it comes to understanding the human (and indeed, ecological) meaning of the economy. That is to say, they quantify the wellbeing of a country's economy – by one measure, at least – but not that of its residents. In 2019, the New Zealand Treasury launched a wellbeing budget, where metrics of citizens' health and wellbeing were employed in assessing policy outcomes.[38] Economic growth was not scrapped altogether, but deprioritised.

In a similar way, theology leads us to argue that we should measure our progress as a society not by how much money we accumulate but by whether people (especially the most vulnerable) are cared for, welcomed and able to belong. In this regard, we ought also to ensure that the environment is at the heart of economic policy in particular moving forward, recognising there is a limit to the planet's resources and costing this in to policy-making accordingly.

1 Perfect, S., *Bridging the Gap*, p.14.

2 Haidt, J., 'Two incompatible sacred values in American universities (text).' *Hayek Lecture Series*, Duke University (2016). Available at: theindependentwhig.com/haidt-passages/haidt/haidt-two-incompatible-sacred-values-in-american-universities/

3 Yates, J. Fractured: *Why Our Societies are Coming Apart and How We Put Them Back Together Again*. (London: Harper Collins, 2021), pp. 17-27.

4 Yates, J. *Fractured*, pp. 123-125, 286-289.

5 Pennington, M. *The Church and Social Cohesion: Connecting Communities and Serving People*. (London: Theos, 2020). Available at: www.theosthinktank.co.uk/cmsfiles/The-Church-and-Social-Cohesion.pdf

6 Fairbairn, C. *Charitable status and independent schools*. (House of Commons Library, 2019, briefing paper 05299). Available at: https://researchbriefings.files.parliament.uk/documents/SN05222/SN05222.pdf

7 Wainwright, O. 'Penthouses and poor doors: how Europe's 'biggest regeneration project' fell flat.' *The Guardian*, 2 February 2021. Available at: www.theguardian.com/artanddesign/2021/feb/02/penthouses-poor-doors-nine-elms-battersea-london-luxury-housing-development

8 Ministry of Housing, Communities and Local Government. *Public attitudes to social housing: Findings from the 2018 British Social Attitudes Survey*. (MHCLG, 2019). Available at: https://assets.publishing.service.gov.uk/government/uploads/system/uploads/attachment_data/file/818535/Public_attitudes_towards_social_housing.pdf

9 Grant, H. and Michael, C. 'Too poor to play: children in social housing blocked from communal playground.' *The Guardian*, 25 March 2019. Available at www.theguardian.com/cities/2019/mar/25/too-poor-to-play-children-in-social-housing-blocked-from-communal-playground

10 Office for National Statistics. *One in eight British households has no garden*. (ONS, 2020). Available at: www.ons.gov.uk/economy/environmentalaccounts/articles/oneineightbritishhouseholdshasnogarden/2020-05-14

11 Joseph Rowntree Foundation. *Impact of poverty on relationships* Available at: www.jrf.org.uk/data/impact-poverty-relationships

12 Jeffreys, B. 'Do children in two-parent families do better?' *BBC News*, 5 February 2019. Available at: www.bbc.co.uk/news/education-47057787

13 Homeless Link. *Why do young people leave home? The bigger picture behind 'family breakdown*. (Homeless Link, 2018). Available at: www.homeless.org.uk/connect/blogs/2018/may/08/why-do-young-people-leave-home-bigger-picture-behind-%E2%80%98family-breakdown%E2%80%99

14 CIPD and High Pay Centre, *FTSE 100 CEO Pay in 2019 and during the pandemic*. (London: High Pay Centre, 2020). Available at: highpaycentre.org/wp-content/uploads/2020/09/FTSE_100_CEO_pay_in_2019_report_WEB.pdf

15 Crim, E., 'The Priest at the End of the Search for a Third Way', *Church Life Journal*, 22 April 2021. Available at: churchlifejournal.nd.edu/articles/the-priest-at-the-end-of-the-search-for-a-third-way/

16 Heales, C., Hodgson, M. and Rich, H. Humanity at Work (London: Young Foundation, 2017) p.47. Available at: youngfoundation.org/wp-content/uploads/2017/04/Humanity-at-Work-online-copy.pdf

17 Hacker, J., 'How to reinvigorate the centre-left? Predistribution' *The Guardian* 12 June 2013 Available at: www.theguardian.com/commentisfree/2013/jun/12/reinvigorate-centre-left-predistribution

18 National Literacy Trust. *Adult Literacy*. Available at: https://literacytrust.org.uk/parents-and-families/adult-literacy/

19 Goodhart, D. *The Road to Somewhere: The New Tribes Shaping British Politics*. (London: Hurst Publishers, 2017).

20 Goodhart, D. *The Road to Somewhere*, p. 163.

21 Alcohol Change UK. *Alcohol Statistics*. Available at: https://alcoholchange.org.uk/alcohol-facts/fact-sheets/alcohol-statistics

22 Gabbatiss, J. 'UK facing 'addiction crisis' as councils cut funding for treatment while alcohol-related deaths soar'. *The Independent*, 11 February 2019. Available at: www.independent.co.uk/news/health/alcohol-deaths-council-funding-cuts-drug-addiction-services-austerity-jonathan-ashworth-a8772301.html

23 Davies, R. 'Only 3% of problem gamblers in UK get help, says study'. *Guardian*, 29 October 2020. Available at: www.theguardian.com/society/2020/oct/29/only-3-of-uk-problem-gamblers-get-proper-help-says-study

24 Coote, A. and Percy, A., *The Case For Universal Basic Services*. (Cambridge: Polity Press, 2020).

25 Calder, S., ''Like the First Step on the Moon': Luxembourg Makes History as First Country with Free Public Transport'. *The Independent*, 29 February 2020. Available at: www.independent.co.uk/travel/news-and-advice/luxembourg-free-travel-train-bus-tram-public-transport-rail-fares-ticket-a9366226.html

26 Pope Francis, *Fratelli Tutti*, § 21.

27 Le Grand, J.,*The case for Universal Basic Capital: a £10k grant for every 18-year-old*. (22 January 2021). Available at: blogs.lse.ac.uk/covid19/2021/01/22/the-case-for-universal-basic-capital-a-10k-grant-for-every-18-year-old/

28 Lansley, S.,. *A Sharing Economy: How Social Wealth Funds Can Reduce Inequality and Help Balance the Books* (Bristol: Policy Press, 2016).

Policy implications and recommendations

29 Detter, D. and Fölster, S., *The Public Wealth of Nations: How Management of Public Assets Can Boost or Bust Economic Growth* (London: Palgrave Macmillan, 2015).

30 Trebeck, K. and Williams, J., *The Economics of Arrival: Ideas for a Grown-Up Economy*. (Bristol: Policy Press, 2019), p. 116.

31 Bickley, P., *People, Place, and Purpose: Churches and Neighbourhood Resilience in the North East* (London: Theos, 2018), p.105. Available at: www.theosthinktank.co.uk/cmsfiles/People-Place-and-Purpose-combined-text-and-cover.pdf

32 Wei, N. 'Why Britain needs a sovereign wealth fund now more than ever'. *Conservative Home* 18 Sept 2021, Available at: www.conservativehome.com/platform/2021/09/nat-wei-why-britain-needs-a-sovereign-wealth-fund-now-more-than-ever.html

33 Godfrey, H., 'Sunak pushes for City of London exemption from G7 tax plan', *CityAM*, 9 June 2021 Available at: www.cityam.com/sunak-pushes-for-city-of-london-exception-from-g7-tax-plan/

34 Guardian Investigation Team. 'Pandora papers: biggest ever leak of offshore data exposes financial secrets of rich and powerful.' *Guardian*, 4 October 2021. Available at: www.theguardian.com/news/2021/oct/03/pandora-papers-biggest-ever-leak-of-offshore-data-exposes-financial-secrets-of-rich-and-powerful

35 Elliott, L., 'UK wealth gap widens in pandemic as richest get £50,000 windfall'. *The Guardian* 12 July 2021. Available at: www.theguardian.com/business/2021/jul/12/uk-wealth-gap-widens-in-pandemic-as-richest-get-50000-windfall

36 Tanner, K. 'Inequality and Finance-Dominated Capitalism: Recommendations for Further Reading.' *Anglican Theological Review* 98 (2016), p.163.

37 Trebeck, K. and Williams, J. *The Economics of Arrival*.

38 Government of New Zealand, *The Wellbeing Being* 30 May 2019. Available at: www.treasury.govt.nz/publications/wellbeing-budget/wellbeing-budget-2019

6. Conclusion

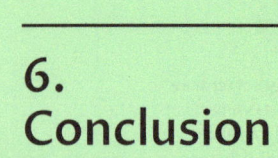

Playing on the linguistic similarity of the words in the Danish language, religious philosopher Søren Kierkegaard wrote that "humanity is human equality" and "inequality is inhumanity"[1]. There is more than a grain of truth in this pun, however, as we have established. The human consequences of excessive inequality are at least as grave as the economic ones, and are profoundly detrimental to our relationships, social connections and ultimately our humanity.

Throughout this project, we have found that perspectives assumed to be at odds with one another on economic matters – in particular those from left and right-wing political positions – find, in the human dimension of inequality, grounds for consensus. Christian theology offers a long-established framework around which this agreement can further be constructed.

As we begin to envision a world beyond the pandemic, influenced by what we have learned about ourselves, our society and our economy during this crisis, we ought also to reconstruct our moral imagination in such a way that a world without excessive economic inequality becomes not only possible, but also unanimously desirable.

1 Kierkegaard, S., *Papers and Journals*: A Selection, translated and edited by Alastair Hannay. (London: Penguin, 1996), p.271. (The Danish word menneskelighed translates as both 'humanity' and 'humaneness' but is formed of *menneske* (human being) and *lighed* (equality, likeness), from which Kierkegaard makes this pun.)

Theos – enriching conversations

Theos exists to enrich the conversation about the role of faith in society.

Religion and faith have become key public issues in this century, nationally and globally. As our society grows more religiously diverse, we must grapple with religion as a significant force in public life. All too often, though, opinions in this area are reactionary or ill informed.

We exist to change this

We want to help people move beyond common misconceptions about faith and religion, behind the headlines and beneath the surface. Our rigorous approach gives us the ability to express informed views with confidence and clarity.

As the UK's leading religion and society think tank, we reach millions of people with our ideas. Through our reports, events and media commentary, we influence today's influencers and decision makers. According to *The Economist*, we're "an organisation that demands attention". We believe Christianity can contribute to the common good and that faith, given space in the public square, will help the UK to flourish.

Will you partner with us?

Theos receives no government, corporate or denominational funding. We rely on donations from individuals and organisations to continue our vital work. Please consider signing up as a Theos Friend or Associate or making a one off donation today.

Theos Friends and Students

— Stay up to date with our monthly newsletter

— Receive (free) printed copies of our reports

— Get free tickets to all our events

£75 / year
for Friends

£40 / year
for Students

Theos Associates

— Stay up to date with our monthly newsletter

— Receive (free) printed copies of our reports

— Get free tickets to all our events

— Get invites to private events with the Theos team and other Theos Associates

£375 / year

Sign up on our website:
www.theosthinktank.co.uk/about/support-us